The Secret Dowry of Eve

The Secret Dowry of Eve

Woman's Role in the Development of Consciousness

Glynda-Lee Hoffmann

Foreword by Joseph Chilton Pearce

Park Street Press
Rochester, Vermont

Park Street Press
One Park Street
Rochester, Vermont 05767
www.InnerTraditions.com

Park Street Press is a division of Inner Traditions International.

Library of Congress Cataloging-in-Publication Data

Hoffmann, Glynda-Lee.
The secret dowry of Eve : woman's role in the development of consciousness / Glynda-Lee Hoffmann ; foreword by Joseph Chilton Pearce.
     p. cm.
Includes bibliographical references.
ISBN 0-89281-968-5 (pbk.)
1. Bible. O.T. Genesis I, 1–IV, 16—Criticism, interpretation, etc.
2. Consciousness—Biblical teaching—Miscellanea. 3. Women—Biblical teaching—Miscellanea. 4. Eve (Biblical figure)—Miscellanea 5. Gematria. 6. Cabala.
I. Title.
  BS1235.52 .H64 2003
  222'.11068—dc21

                              2003001599

Printed and bound in the United States at Lake Book Manufacturing, Inc.

10 9 8 7 6 5 4 3 2 1

Text design and layout by Mary Anne Hurhula
This book was typeset in Bembo, with Beth as a display typeface

Contents

Foreword

This is my third encounter in as many years with Glynda-Lee Hoffmann's remarkable, brilliant, unique, enlightening, intriguing, challenging, and exasperating book. Each revision I have read has been eminently worthwhile, leaving me more richly informed and fascinated as well as irritated and ready to do battle with her. This, then, is no casual read, though it is easy to read, uncomplicated, straightforward, and to the point. Its difficulties have arisen, for me, when it continually overturns my rich heritage of smugly contented masculine sureties and assumptions and my unquestioned and well-knit (if ancient and outmoded) worldview. My conviction that nothing in ancient myth could prove worthwhile to our enlightened electronic minds and world was one of the first assurances that had to go. And such a fuss as Glynda-Lee does generate here, and out of Genesis, mind you, the first book of the Old Testament, with its Adam and Eve, apples and all. Talk about outmoded and ancient! What has such to do with me? This was my first reaction, and it led to my first comeuppance.

Of the Qabalah I knew nothing and cared less. Surely most of us have heard references to it, as we have heard of the I Ching, tarot cards, or the Rig Veda. "Why not read chicken entrails?" was my smart rejoinder. Yet here Hoffmann shows the Qabalah to be a veritable "lens bringing into focus" a worldview of which I knew nothing, though I had long intuited in the foggiest, lazy-minded way. I didn't know that the Qabalah was a "language without cultural associations," as Glynda-Lee makes clear, which was to me an improbable notion since I had just finished a book on the enormous, near-inescapable power of the cultural field effect bending brains and minds to its service. Nor would I

have believed that the Qabalah offered "a cosmic lens perceiving awareness through the activity of . . . cosmic forces . . . beyond the limits of
cultural perspectives, into the realm of the forces that created the brain."
But that the Qabalah offered a way by which the brain could look at
itself, perceive its actions in a new light, and move beyond its limitations
and constraints proved an issue dear to my heart.

Hardly a subject for idle dabbling and amused conjecture, Glynda-
Lee has spent twenty years studying this Qabalah, and in its original
Hebraic language. She has applied her new skill to an analysis of
Genesis—and in its original language too. And the view of this time-
worn myth, given us through Hoffmann's sharp inner eye and the
Qabalah's lens, turns that trite old tale quite upside down and inside out,
and us along with it if we will hang in there. For Glynda-Lee presents
us with a startling picture of how things are in this skull of ours, who we
are, and why we are the way we are—unhappy as that subject might be.

Hoffmann has an admirable grasp of neuroscience and draws on a
cadre of the twentieth century's best, among them Paul MacLean,
Elkhonon Goldberg, and the Damasios. She shows how the "patterns of
cosmology and mythology in Genesis are . . . in line with modern evolutionary theory," giving a graphic picture of the dilemma we are in
today. Her parallels between the two major hemispheres of our neocortex, or new brain, and that famous garden's trees of life and knowledge
are worthy of any mythological treatise. In the same way, she shows how
each of the characters in Genesis represents an archetype of the human
psyche, placing that story of our beginnings in a cosmological framework of creation and evolution that is captivating and compelling. She
offers that the whole sweep of the Genesis story is symbolic of the struggles and conflicts we face within ourselves daily, as we have historically.

A major theme here is her description of our twin tendencies of
continuity, leading to stagnation and despair, and *discontinuity* or disruption, leading to transcendence and newness. Her compelling turnabout
of our ordinary assumption of gender alignments for these tendencies
was a major block in my first reading. That the male is the conservative,

holding back, hedging his bets, building defenses, while the woman is the true liberal, open, trusting, accepting, willing to move into new directions—surely was the reverse of stereotypes. Mine, at least.

Evolution is a major theme in her book, and in another of those neat counterplays she shows how the female is less bound to continuity and more open to movement and growth than the male in his defensive caution. One is reminded of Jesus' observation that the "son of man" (or Adam) has no place to lay his head—and why few of us are willing to take on such an open-ended, unknown role. (The only people I know who have actually done this are women—such as Peace Pilgrim.)

The surprising twist Hoffmann makes concerning Cain and Abel is both an intellectual delight and a sobering point to consider when looking at our fragmented, discordant social scene and chaotic inner life. In no way would I want to take away from the reader his or her discovery of the full sweep of Glynda-Lee's reading on this brotherly conflict and so will say no more. She presents us with an insight that gives new life to this myth, however, even as she reverses all the tired assumptions by which we ignore or counter this extraordinary epic.

Surely there are times when one might be tempted to say Hoffmann takes on a bit too much, tries to explain too much, makes too many side associations that don't always ring true or seem necessary. On the other hand, she gives short shrift to some bones of contention that I, archanarchist even more extravagant in extremities and polemics, have with our contemporary scene. Nevertheless, Glynda-Lee's commentary on our current culture is rich, pithy, and constructive. Certainly she scratches my various itches and rankles of discontent so far as she goes, even as she has gone far beyond most of us on the core issue that counts the most: showing us the wholeness attained by being held in the bonds of love, where those bonds truly lie, and how to open to them.

You will find in what follows here a source of blessing that is sobering and serious, yet there is also novel adventure and enlightening play, at times bordering on fun. Keep it that way and enjoy.

JOSEPH CHILTON PEARCE

Introduction

Origins

One morning thirty years ago, preparing for what I thought would be a trip through the Grand Canyon, I had no idea that in only a few moments I would begin a much more dramatic journey into a psychological and spiritual unknown that would determine my life's trajectory from then on. The first indication that this mysterious, wonderful, and confusing journey had begun was when I walked into my bedroom to begin packing. Immediately an intense feeling of revulsion, complete with stomach-clenching nausea, smacked me with the force of a tidal wave and washed me back out into the hallway. As soon as I was outside the room, the revulsion and nausea evaporated. Poof!

I kept repeating my attempts, with the same results, my brain concluding as Alice (in Wonderland) had, that things were becoming "curiouser and curiouser." Like a driver who sees flashing lights ahead, I stood outside my bedroom door in the hallway trying to figure out how to circumvent the weird roadblock that had suddenly and inexplicably appeared in my path. My rational intention was simplicity itself: Dash into the room, pull out the drawer, dump everything on the bed, stuff it into my traveling bag, and run out of the room with the bag before the sense of revulsion could grab hold of me again. But another force was powerfully present, a *spiritual* force of intention that, at the time, I couldn't name, define, or even recognize, and it had taken over completely.

My intellect, however, had no clue. It had been betrayed so that a break-through could occur, though I was completely unaware of that impending event. I was baffled to the point of oblivion.

The only thing to do in such circumstances, I concluded, is have a cup of tea. I abandoned my attempts to pack and went to see my friend Barbara instead, to relate the bizarre events and seek her guidance over a hot cup of Earl Grey. Barbara and I had been enthusiastically attending some spiritual classes, she for over three years and I for only three weeks. Because she had been going to them so much longer than I, I hoped she might offer some advice. After talking with her awhile, I realized that I didn't want to go to the Grand Canyon, or anywhere else at this particular time in my life, because of my excitement about what I was learning in the classes. But still, I conflictingly felt obligated to make the trip because I'd made a commitment to do so. Barbara had a simple enough solution. She suggested I call Tom, the person I'd made the plans with, and explain my feelings. I made the call right there, from her phone.

As soon as I had explained to Tom the situation and my avid interest in the classes, Barbara suggested something else, something wild and new that she and I had never discussed. She suggested that I invite Tom to join us at class that night. Amazingly—because he had to get on a plane to do this—he agreed. One month later the class morphed into an ashram. It was almost as if the group that had already been together for three years had been waiting for Tom and me to join: Although they had often talked of moving into community together, they didn't actually commit to that idea until Tom and I arrived.

Though the group no longer exists, my journey is still vibrantly alive, for three years into our experiment, the man I originally thought I was going to the Grand Canyon with, but never did, gave me a book instead: *The Cipher of Genesis: The Original Code of Qabala as Applied to the Scriptures,* by Carlo Suares (Shambhala, 1978; Samuel Weiser, 1994). It remains the only text I am aware of that reveals the original Qabalah. Opening the cover of that book was like stepping through a doorway into a spiritual adventure that became a journey through the inner canyons of my mind. It led me to deeply explore the Qabalah, a germ of immensely condensed knowledge that lies buried at the roots of Western civilization.

Most people understand the Qabalah to be a body of Jewish mysticism and theosophy first appearing in the Middle Ages, but in truth it is much more, and much older, reaching all the way back to Genesis. In fact, Genesis is actually a Qabalic text (as are The Song of Solomon, known Qabalically as the Song of Songs or the Quintessence of Quintessences, and the Sephir Yetsira). The Western alphabet is also a derivative of the Qabalah.

What will be made clear in the following chapters is that Genesis is not at all what it appears to be. It is, rather, a coded text with a hidden message, like the hidden purpose of my bout with revulsion that eventually led to my discovery of this ancient text. The Qabalah is the key to discerning the hidden message in Genesis. Through incredibly hard work, exercising and kneading the mind so that it becomes adeptly flexible, pliable, and elastic, able to approach the realm of all possible possibilities, the Qabalah is able to fertilize the visionary elements of our mind.

The way in which the Qabalah induces the mind to germinate its hidden visionary potentials is by offering it a series of symbols to decipher. The term used for a Qabalic symbol is Aut (plural: Autiot). Unlike all other symbols we know, Qabalic symbols do not represent anything. They factually *are* the energy they emit. They are the thing itself. Deciphering the Autiot is like no other exercise. It forces the mind into an unfamiliar realm where it must search around in the dark of the unknown, developing its intuitive and insightful qualities. As those qualities gain strength, they begin to form impressions of the Aut, at first vague and shadowy, like the first layer of a watercolor painting, very indistinct, with imperceptible boundaries. But through persistence and consistently working with the Autiot, clarity eventually arrives. And it arrives with an explosion, as if an inner genie suddenly popped out of a lamp and expanded to an enormous size. Your mind, like the womb of a woman's body, simply stretches and opens up to contain the newly expansive cargo, though you had no idea that such possibilities previously existed. Qabalic meaning is universal yet, paradoxically, gleaning it creates patterns that are completely unlike those we normally follow to process information. By stretching and growing the mind through the study of Qabalah's Autiot, the mind begins to organize itself according to the pattern that Qabalah presents, the pattern of life.

What must be realized is that our minds have been conditioned to perceive through the lens of culture, not the lens of life. It is in learning to make this distinction, the difference between life and culture, that the mind is able to leap the boundaries of the limiting and constricting ideas of culture into the realm of all possible possibilities. Culture is often an intrusion, an imposition, on clarity. Outside of culture's influence, clarity has enormous power.

By studying the Qabalah, I learned that while Genesis has always been regarded as a religious text that is the cornerstone of Judaism, Christianity, and Islam, the power of its hidden message is buried in its mythology. A story about a woman who is crafted from a man's rib, talks to a serpent, and eats fruit that opens her eyes is classic mythology. It speaks to us not of sin, but of hidden possibilities and potentialities.

Wild imagery is typical of myths found in various cultures around the world, such as the story of Athena, who leaps out of her father's forehead, or of the three-headed dog who guards the underground in the myth of Psyche and Eros. Where do such images arise from if not from within the human psyche? And who better to interpret them than the psyche itself? Certainly rationale has little regard for mythic wisdom.

Concerning the psyche, mythology is a repository of rich wisdom; myths are stories that, though appearing magical, inform us of the deepest truths of human essence. Mythological images spring from the deepest recesses of ourselves, unmolested by the culturally shaped intellect. By learning to interpret them, we can reconnect with passions essential to our humanness, passions that guide us to live joyfully and creatively.

On that day thirty years ago, a force that I was completely unaware of was operating to produce those weird feelings of revulsion that prevented me from packing, without which this book would never have been written. It had shown up just as powerfully earlier in my life, but had slipped back below the surface of awareness. That same force drew me into the study of the Qabalah. For the ten years following Tom's gift, I became obsessed with Suares's book. It was my life raft, carrying me safely on my journey, though the seas of cultural confusion roiled through my everyday existence. I was so compelled to read and understand it that nothing else mattered.

Where did that drive, that compelling force, originate? How had it been born in me? When Tom first gave me the book, I had no idea what it contained. Only after I'd begun to master the Qabalah did I develop any sense of its value. Why had I felt so drawn to it right from the beginning, when I was completely ignorant of its hidden jewels?

My studies have convinced me that, in addition to our rational intentions, we are motivated by often hidden spiritual intentions that have the power to instigate a special neurochemistry in the brain that allows us to perceive many of the synchronicities and nonrational forces in our lives. I was being prompted by such intentions to undertake a journey that ultimately led me to discover that the rich mythology of Genesis reveals details about these seldom recognized workings of the human brain, giving us access to their enormous power to change the course of personal and cultural evolution. This book is the fruit of that journey, a fruit like the one Eve shared with Adam. I invite you to share this fruit so your eyes, too, will be opened to clarity, to the pattern of life, and to the recognition of the often strange and unexpected signposts of your own journey of self-discovery.

My inner journey actually began when I was five, with my first lesson from the inner, invisible world.

It was autumn 1955. My family had recently moved into a wonderful old house with enticing nooks and crannies for a five-year-old to explore. A favorite place was my father's study, with its huge fireplace in which, at that moment, a fire was crackling and popping.

Outside, the first storm of the season was brewing. Crimson and gold leaves swirled in the wind. Warm and snug inside the house, with my nose pressed against the cold windowpane, I delighted in knowing I was safe and protected while nature did her best to disrupt our daily lives. Condensation began to collect on the glass, perfect for spontaneous artistry. So absorbed had I become in my finger drawing that I didn't notice the fire dying down until all that remained were iridescent orange coals glowing from its cavernous black center.

My heart sank. I yearned for the flames to leap back to life, with their warmth driving out the chill that had, unnoticed, descended upon the room. As I stood there staring at the blackness, wishing with all my power for a blazing resurrection, an image of my father starting the fire suddenly popped into my head. He poured a small amount of clear liquid on a pile of newspaper, small sticks, and larger pieces of wood. As he struck his match and tossed it onto the pile, flames instantly shot up.

Aha! I knew exactly what to do. If a small amount of liquid did the job, a large amount would surely be better.

I ran to the kitchen, got the biggest glass I could find, and filled it to the brim with water. As I poured the liquid on the coals, expecting the flames to leap and dance the way I had envisioned, I was not prepared for the reality that presented itself. My anticipated joy fell with a thud, as the soggy, smoking, smelly mess of ash hissed a last dying breath.

I stared at the grisly scene for what seemed like an eternity. Then a voice inside my head spoke very clearly and with deep authority: "Things are not what they appear to be."

Yo.

It would be thirty years before I knew with certainty that my early experience pointed to how the brain processes information, particularly how we frame new data with old memories to learn something previously unknown. I would discover, during those thirty years, that the brain's ability to process information clearly is often compromised by more than we might imagine, by our attitudes, traditions, expectations, beliefs, and linguistic habits. This compromising of clarity leads to a myriad of social, psychological, and scientific errors, evident in our tendency to produce toxic environments and toxic relationships.

Our ignorance about the internal world of awareness is what causes us so much undefined misery and suffering, the so-called human problem. If this ignorance of the brain were illuminated and enlightened, we would be very different individuals—wiser, happier, and kinder—who would create much different societies—less restrictive, less toxic, less violent, less deceptive. The power to build heaven on earth sits squarely on our own shoulders, quite literally, and will inevitably grow as we educate ourselves about that mysterious three pounds of tissue between our ears: the human brain and its hidden spiritual qualities. As Carl Jung once said, "Who looks outside dreams. Who looks inside awakens."

Surprisingly, all this was recorded thousands of years ago in Genesis, but it was misunderstood precisely for the reasons I have outlined: Those who read and interpreted it did so without any knowledge of how the brain processes information. As a consequence, like Galileo, we have been imprisoned in our own house of consciousness, limited in our scope of study and impelled to adhere to obsolete ideas, even though our potential for self-discovery is as powerful as any telescope.

Genesis is a completely misunderstood text because originally it was not linguistic. That's a lot of information to grasp in the short amount of time it takes to read it, so let me say it another way: Genesis is a coded text. It was not meant to be read in a linear fashion. One way this can be recognized is that it doesn't make much sense. First of all, there are two confusing stories that somehow blend into each other. Genesis 1 gives us the Six Days of Creation story. Genesis 2, 3, and 4 give us the Garden of Eden story. Religion has tried to make sense of it by taking the words literally, but it doesn't work. There are simply too many inconsistencies, contradictions, and confusing riddles. You may ask, if Genesis was not written to make rational sense, why was it written at all? Perhaps it was to awaken hidden potential in the brain, potential that lies dormant if we accept the text at face value, much as our under-standing of our world and solar system remains dormant if we accept that the Earth is standing still simply because to our senses it appears to do so.

Genesis is not about a first man and woman; it is about potentiality and possibility, the properties of light now being defined by quantum physics but which have existed all along, hidden from our collective awareness because our cultural mind has been too rigid to see them. The story begins with the creation of light on the first day and follows the pattern of evolution, culminating with human beings. Later, on the seventh day, after eating the famous fruit, Adam and Eve's eyes are opened. Does this not reveal a hidden relationship, associating light with insight, outer light with inner light?

Quantum scientists have proved that light does not behave accord-ing to the old Newtonian laws of matter. Light is a substance with its own laws, and our perception of those laws changes the perception of reality that traditional science has been built upon. This is just as true for inner light. Indwelling light has all the possibility and potentiality that quantum analysis reveals. That field of possibility is inner: psycho-logical, spiritual, and neurological. Awareness, according to the Qabalah, is the action of light processing information inside the human brain. It is our eyes that respond to light and it is light—inner light—that fertilizes expansive awareness in us, ergo enlightenment.

Insight, because it is dictated by the laws of light, is the *fire* of aware-ness. It is the same light referred to in John 1:5, "And the light shineth in the darkness and the darkness comprehended it not." All of us—not just Jesus—are endowed with this inner light of insight. He was emphatic about stating that, but he also said we need to get the logs out of our eyes in order to recognize it. Things are not what they appear to be. Insight is a power that helps us recognize authenticity.

Religions, specifically Judaism, Christianity, and Islam, all have one common flaw. They are all patriarchal *interpretations* of scriptures—that is, the legitimacy of their interpretations is based solely on *assumed* male authority. The word *patriarchy* literally means the "hierarchy of priests" who were referred to as "Fathers," a hierarchy that filtered down to the secular level, with family fathers assuming the role of decision makers. Likewise, "the father of our country" and "the father of the scientific method" became phrases of recognition. That pattern has resulted today in a general assumption of male authority, and the assumption that society needs authorities to keep chaos from erupting. This is one of those beliefs that obscure clarity. It has effectively limited, and in some cases actually destroyed, a vast knowledge about feminine power, creating an enormous void in awareness while it has simultaneously allowed authorities everywhere to misuse the power invested in their positions, even at the highest levels.

At this point, I would like to clarify even further the use of the term *patriarchy* in the following pages, making a distinction between it and *masculinity* to ensure that my intent is not to male-bash. Patriarchy is much different from masculinity. Patriarchy, a social system of domination that arose as men of power needed a way to protect their assets, grew out of ownership—a man's wife, children, and slaves were at one time (and in some places still are) considered his property. Masculinity, on the other hand, is the essence of maleness, which often manifests as protection. Stronger males are called on to protect weaker females and children. Through time, patriarchy distorted the natural behavior of masculine protection into masculine domination. The masculine function of a protective husk became, in the pattern of patriarchy, overbearing and intent on stunting the growth of the germ. The term *patriarchy* as used here refers to social organization, not masculine identity.

Patriarchal perception focuses attention outward, yet all awareness takes place within. Religious authorities have for centuries used this outward focus to frighten people into believing in a God of retribution who punishes sinners at death by sending them to hell. Such beliefs are based on the assumption that God lives outside the human realm somewhere, as an authority over human life. The story in Genesis has been interpreted as one that takes place in the outer world, as history, because this is the traditional, patriarchal theme that has been supported for centuries by religious authorities. But what if it were not meant to convey information pertaining to the outer world, or to any assumed outer authorities? What if, instead, Genesis were a story that not only takes place in the inner world, but actually also defines and describes that inner world so perfectly it can now be verified by scientific analysis? And what if it were this inner world, when it becomes sufficiently developed, that is supposed to act as our authority?

Leonard Shlain explains—in his book *Art and Physics: Parallel Visions in Space, Time and Light* (William Morrow and Co., 1991)—that a new way of looking at the world always precedes a new way of thinking about the world. Historically, all new waves of thought have been preceded by new waves of art. Quantum physics was preceded by modern abstract art, the classical art of ancient Greece preceded its ideal philosophers, the Renaissance began with art. Indeed, all of human civilization seems to have followed on the heels of the exquisite cave art produced thirty to forty thousand years ago.

If we wish to overcome the limitations of patriarchal civilization, with its accompanying violence, toxicity, and deception, we must, as Shlain points out, realize that our neural ability to process new ideas is dependent upon first being able to process new imagery. New ways of seeing precede new ways of thinking. In other words, as far as the neural processing of new information is concerned, *seeing* is supreme, because light is activated at its most potentially fertile level, inside the human brain. In Gensis, eating the apple *opens the eyes* of Adam and Eve.

Mythology is storytelling through imagery. Words are used to create the images. But the images are primary, not the words. Mythology is a language of images created by the psyche. Such imagery often visits us in dreams, when the mind is freed from its daytime interpretations, which have been wrapped in the sequencing of linear time. The vivid imagery of Genesis is what makes it so captivating. By viewing it through its imagery we open up our brain's interpretive mechanisms and learn to see in new ways. As its title implies, this may be the original purpose of Genesis. A genesis is the birth of something new. It is a new beginning, a generating of new life, new opportunities, new potential, new fecundity.

By reframing Genesis as mythology, we expand our awareness and enlarge our perception. This activates generative forces at work in the brain and psyche, forces we seldom think about, yet which have an impact on us every day of our lives, because the mythology of Genesis is no ordinary mythology. It is shaped and molded by the extraordinary teaching of Qabalah. This ancient teaching, which has never been fully understood, contains the knowledge of the pattern of whole systems: the pattern of life. It has the power to transform us through our own clarity, allowing us to see previously hidden relationships crucial to our understanding of life, ourselves, and especially our marvelous brain.

Forty thousand years ago human societies were much different from how they are today, for one specific reason: They were guided by shamans who derived their information from the inner realms of awareness and intuition, motivated by pure intentions. The shamans used trancelike experiences induced through sound, psychedelic plants, and ritual to discover information that was necessary for survival or simply for happier living, information guiding, for example, the delivery of a breech baby or the healing of a conflict between parents and a child. The inner journeys of the shamans were the factors that allowed early human societies to thrive in a world full of danger because the shamans' intentions were pure and their powers of intuition were nurtured. The shamanic experience is an inner one, deriving information from a powerful inner source through pure intention. Each of us is endowed with this power, inside the human brain. But in order for us to utilize it, we must recognize and develop it, motivated by our pure intentions for self-discovery. As Henri Poincaré pointed out, "It is through science that we prove, but through intuition that we discover."

In the brain, neural networks carry all the energy used to process information: any information, all information. These networks carry the payload of perceiving, understanding, and interpreting all data and all symbols. The brain self-generates its neural networks by recognizing, accumulating, and integrating patterns. These patterns are what we know as information. Nobel Prize–winning psychologist Herbert Simon believes that learning involves the accumulation of easy-to-recognize patterns of all kinds. These accumulated patterns of information are represented by maps of neural networks in the brain. The trouble is, some patterns of information are not so easily recognized. Sometimes we can't see the forest for the trees.

Many of these patterns that we still do not recognize, that cause us enormous misery, are inherent in personal and social interactions orchestrated by patriarchal attitudes and values inherent in authoritarian social organization. Most people today do not experience misery and suffering because of natural disasters such as floods, earthquakes, and fires (though some still do). Most people experience misery because other people inflict it upon them—or because they inflict it upon themselves—through predatory attitudes and practices inherent in the authoritarian social structure on which patriarchy depends. Our failure to recognize these patterns leaves us blind. There are no neural networks. This area—personal and social interaction—is mediated by one portion of the brain that has not been fully developed in most of us. She is the Cinderella of our internal world, waiting for the fairy godmother of our own recognition to dress her up and send her to the ball. Insight is the sudden recognition of a pattern of information that previously had been unrecognized and therefore unknown. The pattern existed; we simply did not recognize it, like gravity before Newton. This is what the story in Genesis teaches us, to open our inner eyes so that we can recognize patterns of information in our lives to which we are currently blind.

Pattern recognition is critical to science, when researchers suddenly *see* a pattern that had been there all along yet remained undetected. Katy Payne is a scientist who has made considerable contributions to the study of elephants. She discovered that elephants transmit sounds that we cannot hear—infrasounds or subsounds—too low for human ears to detect.

Her discovery is a perfect example of pattern recognition revealing hidden relationships through insight that offers us critical information.

Payne spent several days sitting next to an elephant pen at the zoo, jotting down notes about the animals' behavior. Shortly afterward she got on a plane. As the plane started up, she experienced the low series of vibrations normal to jet aircraft and suddenly realized that she had experienced those same low vibrations while sitting next to the elephant pen, but had not recognized them until they were produced by the plane. In a flash of insight she realized that the elephants must have been creating sounds too low for human ears to detect, sounds they used to communicate with each other. She then designed a series of experiments that later proved her hypothesis. This is the power of pattern recognition and insight. They can change everything by changing the way we *see*.

Once the brain recognizes a new pattern, a domino effect often rockets through its interior landscape, reshaping neural maps by connecting and reorganizing them in new, more powerful ways. The impact of neural reorganization and integration through insight is captured by a famous scene in *The Miracle Worker*, a play and film dramatizing the early chaotic life of Helen Keller, left blind and deaf at the age of nineteen months by a mysterious illness. In the scene, Helen's teacher, Annie Sullivan, is grasping Helen's hand under flowing water, repeatedly spelling out the word *water* in Helen's tiny palm. Angry and uncomprehending, Helen struggles, resisting Annie's attempts to instruct her. Suddenly the light of insight pierces Helen's darkness. Awareness cascades through her brain like the water rushing over her hands. Instantly she perceives what only a moment before she could not: that the water has a name. The unknown becomes known because the pattern Annie signed is *recognized,* not by Helen's eyes, but instead by interpretive mechanisms in her brain.

Helen is ecstatic. She spells the name back into Annie's hand for confirmation. In the next moment, as the light of insight radiates throughout her mind, Helen realizes that everything must have a name.

Her entire world instantly begins to reorganize itself into meaning through pattern recognition, out of the chaos and fragmentation that had previously been her experience. She races around the yard demanding greedily that Annie spell all those glittering names into her palm. Her neural networks are on fire with new awareness. They are connecting and integrating at a furious rate because Annie had spent several months laying the groundwork for this anticipated moment of pattern recognition.

If Annie hadn't insisted, for all those months previously, on signing into Helen's palm, creating the impulses in her brain that Helen would later recognize and interpret as a pattern of information, nothing would have happened. Helen's brain *learned to see* that things have names, using insight to recognize previously undetected patterns of information. Her brain, though she didn't know it, had been constructing a series of neural networks, all in relationship to one another, in response to Annie's signing of patterns into her palm.

Annie's palm signings prompted Helen's brain to organize meaning out of chaos. Those *seemingly* random signings (they seemed random to Helen) suddenly connected up through insight. A series of neural networks in Helen's brain had self-generated, finally allowing her to *interpret* what she had assumed were random gestures into a formal pattern. What had been incomplete in Helen's mind was now whole, and she had a new power at her disposal, the power of communication, which had been halted at nineteen months.

Although Helen's sight and hearing had been intact until her illness, she had no literacy—no awareness that labels can be written down using specific groups of symbols for sounds. Hearing words as we do when we are young is a much different neural activity from writing or reading them. Not only did Helen's brain have to bridge a gap of several years during which she heard and saw nothing, but it also had to bridge the gap of literacy. Miraculously, because of the brain's enormous plasticity and because of Annie Sullivan's unwavering determination, Helen's brain was able to move into new territory, building neural networks where none had existed previously.

If we want to be whole, we must learn to use insight to recognize and interpret the hidden relationships between our internal states of awareness and our external behaviors. This is the information we need to be whole. The brain will then build neural networks that connect what had previously been unconnected so that our intentions produce the actions, and responses, we want. As we self-generate new connections between neurons in the brain, the brain's structure changes and our ability to see expands. New neural connections often have remarkable effects on other aspects of the brain, such as altering its neurochemistry. Changes in the brain's structure and function are demonstrated through what we commonly refer to as personal, psychological, and spiritual growth. We can't see this growth, we can't taste it, smell it, hear it, or touch it. The fact remains, however, that without neural growth there is no personal growth. This growth does not arise from any outer power. No one can give it to us or bestow it upon us. We each self-generate it by fertilizing the subatomic level of light in the brain, where all possible possibilities await us.

Qabalah does for the brain what Annie's signings did for Helen. It promotes the development of insight by tapping the Autiot into neural substance. Information in the Autiot—that of hidden relatinships in whole systems—is carried along. The central relationship of all whole systems is an integration of opposites, such as the integration of germ and husk in every seed. Husk and germ together provide the essential pattern of wholeness, an integration of opposites. This pattern existed prior to the formation of seeds; indeed, it dictates the structure of all seeds. The power of growth is encapsulated in germs, not husks. In us, the germ of growth is the internal, *feminine* element of awareness, whereas the husk is the external, *masculine* element of behavior. The germ energy within us has the power to redesign its husk, its container of behavior. If the interplay between psyche and behavior is allowed to develop authentically, it will naturally lead to self-growth and maturity. But in patriarchal societies, outer authorities have been substituted for one's inner germ of awareness, which is why patriarchy cannot evolve and why we are, essentially, socially and psychologically static, mirroring Adam's state of awareness before Eve is created in the Genesis mythology.

Although the pattern of integrated opposites so clearly defined in a seed is extolled in many myths, such as the story of Isis and Osiris, in which Isis re-creates Osiris from the parts of his body that have been dispersed after his death, it has been obscured in patriarchal paradigms. Patriarchy has its foundations in hierarchy and authority, one gender having more power than the other, males over females. But there is no hierarchy between a germ and a husk. They work together or they don't work at all. In the brain, fertility is released when the feminine is recognized, as in the love story between a photographer and an ordinary housewife in *The Bridges of Madison County*. He saw her, and she needed to be seen, to be recognized and valued. It's a classic story of the relationship between the masculine and the feminine in the psyche, between recognition and fertility of thought. Why else would such a simple story captivate us so?

Too often, in our culture of static social authority, inner awareness is not allowed to assert itself. Social values, attitudes, and laws—*external* forces—are relied on to control behavior and dictate the course of culture. In such societies, humans are left incomplete, without either the knowledge of wholeness or its application to human personal and social endeavors. The feminine side of our humanity has been devalued and denied by patriarchal perception. The result is that most of us, women and men alike, now have overly masculinized psyches. We have become like Adam in Genesis, able to name all the animals—a metaphor for naming and defining what is outside of us and came before us, what is obvious to the senses—but unable to name or define our helpmate, our inner, feminine realm of awareness, inner light, hidden potentiality, and possibility. This lack of awareness concerning our inner (feminine) realm is mirrored in patriarchal attitudes toward women and what they contribute to society.

Evidence of this lack can be seen in our attitudes toward pleasure.

Most of us have no idea what actually pleases us. We've lost touch with a component in our psyche that measures such things. Take, for instance, the ratings for films. Violence is given a G or PG rating, but sex leads to an R or X rating. In other words, pain is allowed but not pleasure. Most of our fundamental religious views of sex are based on puritan ideals that uphold the necessity of pain in controlling people's behavior, and especially in controlling their pleasure in sexuality.

Adam, in Genesis, presents a picture of the patriarchal intellect whose educational agenda, passed down from Greek and Roman authorities, has remained relatively unchanged for the past few thousand years. He has lost his sense of wholeness and of pleasure, whether he lives within men or women. He is what needs to change so the new world of wholeness can be born, so a potential heaven can be fertilized from within. He needs to lose his insistence on hierarchy and outer authorities and embrace the universal pattern, germs and husks, the pleasure of integrated opposition. For this, we need a new vision that unfolds from within.

A story that points to this situation is one many of us learned as children, about the five blind men and the elephant. Each of the blind men, representing one of the five senses, defines the elephant according to only one part of its body. None sees the enormous elephantine truth of life, its wholeness.

The blind men represent the limitations of the senses, their inability to perceive the hidden relationships in whole systems. If we rely on superficial perception and the abstract ideas we formulate from it, we can never attain our own wholeness because, like the blind men, we do not *see* it. Only when the powers of perception are focused inward, and inner light illuminates awareness, does a new level of perception begin to build itself. All of this is present in Eve's story. The path of recovery, the journey to wholeness, is in revaluing the feminine and integrating the two opposites psychologically, according to the universal pattern.

The Qabalic mythology of Genesis teaches us to recognize the relationships inherent in wholeness, information that is not usually presented in academic institutions, secular or nonsecular. Human ideology is just barely beginning to consider the nature of whole systems. The Qabalah was perceived thousands of years ago, probably by the shamans of those times. Yet it remains a mystery today because it must be perceived initially by the image-processing functions of the brain, not the linguistic functions, and until quite recently all knowledge in our civilization was passed on solely through literacy processed by the linguistic left hemisphere.

Indeed, three of the world's major religions utilize the reading of sacred texts by males as rites of passage. Male religious authorities became obsessed with the written word, a testament to the literate left hemisphere's tendency to dominate the neural processing of information the way patriarchal men tend to dominate women. When this occurs—when the brain's information-processing systems are subject to the narrow confines of a literate, linguistic, authoritarian intellect, and are denied access to the vast realm of image-laden information accessible to them—the intellect becomes rigid, restrictive, and inflexible. Traditional religious interpretations of our sacred scriptures have subjected us to a neural wasting disease brought on by patriarchal attitudes held firmly in place by our habit of employing androcentric and authoritarian linguistics. We need to unshackle the arrested Galileo in our minds and allow a new vision, a new possibility, to fertilize our awareness.

The Qabalists who wrote the Genesis story were intent on germinating the brain's enormous capacities. In order for the literate brain to gain more flexibility, it had to be restricted from investigating certain kinds of information until it could establish a neural network capable of interpreting the information clearly. In the story, Adam is restricted from eating the fruit of the tree of the knowledge of good and evil. The reason he is restricted from this particular fruit isn't because it is imperative that man obey God—a typical patriarchal interpretation—but rather because his brain isn't ready for it yet, just as a three-year-old's brain isn't ready for trigonometry.

When we view the Genesis story through the lens of Qabalic mythology, we bypass linguistic habits that shackle us to impotent neural processes and instead fertilize the image-processing centers in the brain to give us more choices. The brain's incredible fertility then begins to generate new neurons and new connections, germinating new patterns that provide new ways of seeing for new ways of thinking.

By telling of a man and woman whose eyes are opened, Genesis offers us the supreme message of wholeness. Like Sleeping Beauty awakening from her hundred-year slumber, the eye-opening of Adam and Eve is a beautiful portrayal of the deep role that *recognition* and *interpretation* play in our journey of growth and self-discovery. Recognition and interpretation contain enormous hidden inner (neurological) power—germ power—for personal growth.

The human psyche is where the kingdom of heaven is located, the kingdom of (potential) wholeness within us. As we will see, in that kingdom Adam is the one who names; he names all the animals and later names Eve. But it is Eve who brings the fire of insight. She is the first to eat the fruit that opens their eyes. She sees that it is the fruit of wholeness: It erupts from the blossom that was produced by the tree that grew from the seed that embodies the integrated pair of opposites, germ and husk. In that vision of wholeness she restores Adam's fragmented and incomplete perception, saving him from the psychological rigidity that had previously held him captive.

A realization of the oppressive characteristics of a static authoritarian mind is fundamental to understanding the Qabalah. How we interpret events is how we frame them. A classic example is the difference between framing life as a process of evolution (dynamic growth and change) and framing it through creationism (static ideology). The story in Genesis is one in which the *disruption* of a rigid mind is paramount, because disruption fertilizes new potential and fecundity. In the traditional framing of this story—which has governed, to a large extent, our religious and cultural perspective for the past three thousand years—Eve is condemned for instigating the eye-opening event. Yet *mythologically* she neither existed in the remote past, nor committed any sin, nor even tempted Adam. Rather, according to the mythology, she *saves* him, as Beauty saves the Beast and the Princess saves the Frog.

Such feminine images are abundant in mythology. They represent the psyche's trustworthy germing power, its hidden, self-generating fertility. Far from being "fallen," or any type of sinner, Eve—germ power—is what saves us from falling into static (beastly) behavior. Her deep knowledge of wholeness, of self-growth, discovery, and clarity, are the keys to paradise, her secret dowry bequeathed to each of us.

Growth, from incompleteness to wholeness, is the real subject of Genesis, the premier myth of our culture. According to the Qabalic interpretation of Genesis, the events that take place in the story are not historical or religious accounts; they are metaphors of the psyche's struggles to empower its growth processes. Mythology is the timeless container for this story. It does not arise from the linear dimensions of time and space, nor from the human dimensions of reason and rationale. It is eternal and transcendent. In a word, it is sacred. Adam and Eve are mythological and psychological archetypes, alive in each of us. When they eat the fruit that opens their eyes—the eyes of recognition, insight, and clarity—the static elements of the mind are transformed into dynamic elements of growth.

Our current understanding of the psyche and the role that myth plays in the growth of its self-knowledge; our widespread literacy; and our ability to keep current with the most recent research into human brain structure, function, and process all converge at a point of cultural readiness that makes a widespread understanding of the original Qabalic intent in Genesis as possible as it is necessary.

The Secret Dowry of Eve is one step toward that goal. Introducing Genesis as a story written according to Qabalic mythology, it reveals a classic hero's journey as a metaphor of psychological growth and spiritual integration. In this story the brain and psyche journey through an exploration of their own contents. During that exploration, they integrate their fragmented knowledge base with feelings and emotions, creating an enormous potential for clarity and the hidden visionary elements of the mind in order to achieve wholeness. This self-organized wholeness reveals all errors, heals all wounds, and destroys all illusions within the psyche so that creativity and joy can be our daily experience. Only from such joy and creativity can heaven be built on earth.

And so I invite you on a journey of self-discovery and wholeness, a journey depicted in the metaphor of the enslaved Hebrews freed from bondage in Egypt. We are the Hebrews, enslaved to patriarchal paradigms of dominance, obedience, and punishment. Genesis portrays this extraordinary inner journey to wholeness and pleasure through its rich mythology, revealing details about the human brain seldom recognized, but which have enormous power to fertilize personal and cultural evolution. Supported with findings of brain research and distinguished from traditional interpretations, this is clearly *not* the Genesis we think we know so well. It is, rather, an interactive story for the brain that reads it, promoting personal growth and spiritual awakening as the Qabalah intended.

The first two chapters of this book explore the cosmological narrative of Genesis 1 and the shift in Genesis 2 to the mythological depiction of events in the Garden of Eden.

The third chapter presents an overview of the four neural structures of the brain, their link to attitudes and behavior patterns, and the role played by the psychological integration of these four structures in fostering growth into our full human potential.

The fourth, fifth, and sixth chapters are a guidebook to the hero's journey portrayed in Genesis 2, 3, and 4, making the path to integration accessible to all.

Important note: Before beginning Chapter 1, please take a few minutes to study the graph, chart, and accompanying text in appendix 1. This appendix offers information and advice on beginning your study of the Qabalah, including sources of information on translation and a method for undertaking study. Familiarizing yourself with its material before you read on, and referring back to it as we translate the Hebrew in Genesis Qabalically thoughout our discussion will help you as the next chapters unfold. The original Qabalah is presented, complete with its numbers and names, along with Carlo Suares's definitions for the first nine archetypes and their relationships to the other fourteen symbols (which took him forty arduous years to re-create). Suares warns that the Qabalah cannot be distorted or perverted, but it can be lost and has been lost and resurrected several times throughout our history. Its resurfacing is highly dependent upon the desire of human beings to know truth. When that desire is strong enough, the Qabalah presents itself, deposits its information, then plunges again into the unknown.

Appendix 2 offers a deeper exploration of the sacred alphabet through the remarkable work of Stan Tenen and the Meru Foundation.

Before we begin our journey, you might find it both helpful and illuminating to read appendix 1 in order to gain a better understanding of the Autiot that appear in the following chapters.

So now, let the journey begin.

1

The Six Days of Creation

Several years ago, when our three daughters were all still young enough to enjoy the same movie, we decided a family outing was needed to lift the doldrums of a winter afternoon. *Beauty and the Beast* was showing at the local theater. As we headed out, albeit still tying shoelaces and making sure the dog was inside the house, my husband realized his hat was missing, so a last-minute search for the hat began. As I was looking under sofa cushions, our youngest daughter, Jenny, pointed to her dad's head and said in the one-word sentences typical of eighteen-month-old toddlers, "Up." Daddy picked her up and said something like, "Yeah, Daddy needs his hat." Jenny replied, "Up," again. We all validated her contribution to our search, but the hat was still missing. My husband put her down and we resumed the search. Jenny, who has proved to be as persistent through the years, pointed to her dad's head once again and again repeated, "Up." By this time, we were all a bit frazzled. Jenny realized we weren't getting her message so she took more drastic measures. Grabbing her father by the hand, she dragged him into the closet and pointed up. There on the top shelf was his hat.

It's now obvious to me that my daughter could clearly see the hat in her mind and was assuming that when she said, "Up," we could see it too. She had no idea that her communication of the word *up* didn't carry all the information she assumed it did. Yet at eighteen months she was able to figure that out and find another way to get her message across.

Adults aren't always so astute. Assumptions about how we process information are still the cause of incalculable misunderstandings. Sociolinguist Deborah Tannen has studied the way men and women engage in conversations and concludes—in her best-selling book *You Just Don't Understand: Women and Men in Conversation* (Quill, 2001)— that the different genders use different though equally valid communication styles. Tannen discovered that when women engage in conversation, the primary reason is to gather information. By contrast, when men engage in conversation, the primary reason is to detect and upgrade their social status. Problems occur when we make assumptions about how others are interpreting the information we give them, so feedback is essential if we truly want to understand each other.

Genesis presents a similar problem. Most of us are familiar with the words and stories of its first four chapters, regardless of our religious affiliation. They have been passed from parents to children, from rabbis, priests, and ministers to congregations, and from teachers to students for countless generations. If we wish to see the true depths of these stories, however, revealing a powerful secret about human awareness, we must reexamine the familiar assumptions with which we interpret them. Unrecognized assumptions are an enormous part of traditional interpretations of Genesis, which insist that we frame it as fall/redemption theology, ergo history. To see Genesis through such a lens, however, is to miss the whole point of the story. Perhaps we were even set up to make those erroneous assumptions so that when we finally discover the truth, it helps us realize how wrong we can be, inducing us to be more humble when approaching sacred texts. Realizing how wrong we can be about any number of things is part of the process of self-awareness and transformation. How we perceive and frame information is often based on our own peculiar dysfunctions and concerns, rather than on any truth, as the following story of my old friend Bill illustrates.

When I was in my early twenties, living in an intentional community of people who had come together to study personal evolution, a man named Bill tended the garden. Bill was the quiet type who went about his duties with focus and intention, rarely talking to others. I got to know him because we were houseparents together, in charge of fourteen children. One day, when Bill was in the garden, as usual, preparing a bed for planting, one of the kids walked by and mentioned that she'd overheard a conversation in the office about Bill receiving a telephone call from a "Jane somebody." Bill's ears pricked up immediately. "Jane called!" he said to himself. His thoughts ran on: "Oh hallelujah! Now I can leave this hellhole."

Bill had been having trouble lately. He'd been with us for about a year, and as is typical of our pattern, he had begun to run into his own resistance. This resistance can show up in many ways, but for Bill it showed up as a desire to leave the community as soon as possible. The call from Jane was his ticket out. Jane had been his girlfriend, but a year earlier he had left her because their relationship had become so unbearably emotional that he simply couldn't take it any more. After a year of separation, however, their dysfunction didn't seem so clear to him; he could remember only that he loved her and wanted to try again. These thoughts traveled at lightning speed through his brain within half a second of hearing the message that Jane had called.

Bill raced down the hill to the office and began to inquire about the message. Someone told him that Barbara had taken it, so he began a frantic search for Barbara. She wasn't in the office at that moment, so he looked in the kitchen, then in the laundry, then finally he looked in her room, where I was sitting with her, having a cup of tea. He dashed into the room, sweaty and heaving, and asked, "Barbara, did you take a phone call for me?"

Barbara was a bit perplexed by Bill's anxiety, because he had never exhibited any for the entire year he'd been with us. Tentatively she replied, "Yes, Jane called. She said your seeds are in."

Jane was a woman Bill had spoken with over the phone, ordering seeds for the garden. When he'd heard the message that Jane had called, his mind had instantly jumped to his old girlfriend because of his state of unhappiness. It had never occurred to him that another Jane might call.

When Bill realized what he'd done, how wrong he'd been, his mind collapsed and he toppled over like a pillar crashing to the ground. Barbara and I were stunned. We just sat there, staring, with our mouths open. We'd never witnessed such behavior from Bill and had no idea what had just occurred to precipitate it. As we were staring, Bill raised his head and said ruefully, "I played such a trick on myself." It was later he filled me in on the details.

Much like Bill's perception of or interpretation of the call from Jane was colored by his own unresolved issues with his old girlfriend, our perceptions of Genesis and the information it relates are often colored by our personal and cultural perspectives, however dysfunctional.

Mythologically, Genesis is about our neurology, not our history, and its depiction of human neurology can now be verified by solid scientific fact. Rather than depicting outer events, the imagery of Genesis depicts the inner realm of neurological structure and function. What is more, it may be telling us that the power of our own awareness can affect, alter, and even enlarge our neurology.

This is the power of personal transformation. It is determined not by events observed in a laboratory, but by events observed within one's own mind. It is quantum mechanics at the personal level, because it involves observing the behavior of light—inner light—in the processing of information. "Man, know thyself" were the words chiseled into the Delphic Oracle. How can we know ourselves if we do not observe our inner world? Ironically, for "man," the inner world is the realm of the feminine, and it is the woman in Genesis who initiates the journey into this inner world. On our own journeys we must not allow ourselves to be put off, diverted, or deluded by interpretations from various authorities. Remember: There is no better authority on your inner world than you.

QABALAH'S UNIFYING FACTOR

The key to understanding Genesis lies in the sacred teaching of Qabalah, which reveals hidden relationships in whole systems, such as those between the opposites of husk and germ. Within that relationship, it is the germ that contains vital potential, the quality of fertility, represented in Genesis by Eve.

Germ energy is the womb of human potential. Culturally that potential has manifested mostly through technological development because social patterns have been dictated by patriarchy. Masculine outer interests—territory and technology—now dominate cultural institutions. What we need in order to balance our progress in technological development is a similar progression of our inner social, psychological, and spiritual development.

Women are generally better than men at perceiving the relationships in whole systems, especially whole social systems (which have their roots in whole psychological systems). This is due both to the design of the brain itself (elaborated in chapter 3) and to the relationship between every mother and her children. Although such relationships are often portrayed as deeply emotional, they actually involve, at their very core, the quintessential human talent for problem solving, which leads to trust. Eve, in Genesis, represents this feminine problem-solving fertility in the human psyche, and is appropriately referred to as a "helpmate."

A mother with a crying infant is a mother with a problem in need of a solution. If she does not find that solution, and quickly, she is in danger of losing her wits because a crying baby can work havoc on the nervous system of its mother. So good mothers, by necessity, become good (fertile) problem solvers. And the problems they become good at solving are the problems of whole systems, because the interactions between mother and infant form a whole social system.

A baby offers instant feedback, an essential ingredient for self-organization in whole systems. If mother solves baby's problem, baby will immediately settle down and begin loving mother appropriately because by solving the problem mother proves she is capable and trustworthy. If mother does not solve baby's problem, baby's crying and screaming will often escalate until things are unbearable. This is how infants train their mothers to be trustworthy and capable problem solvers and this is how women become good at solving problems that arise due to the relationships inherent in whole systems.

As we will see, Adam is a man with a problem, which, like most of our problems, is rooted in errors of interpretation due to a lack of (feminine) knowledge about relationships and feedback in whole systems. The story in Genesis depicts Eve as emerging out of Adam's rib because she is a part of him—initially such a tiny, hidden part that he cannot recognize her, so the story enlarges her, as a biology textbook enlarges the image of a cell so that we can recognize details we might not otherwise notice.

In a classic tale of recovering wholeness that takes place within the human psyche, *not* in some remote idealized past, Adam is rescued by this unrecognized and devalued feminine part of himself. Only then does he name her Eve, "the mother of all living." Her role is that of archetypal fertile mother—fertile with possibilities—and only when he recognizes this can he name her. Plato voiced much the same sentiment when he declared, "Give me a new mother and I'll give you a new world!"

Qabalah maintains that all growth everywhere, whether of the stars or of human consciousness, is based on one pattern: an interplay or relationship—a feedback loop—between a pair of opposites such as heaven and earth, night and day, light and darkness. The pattern is referred to in Qabalic literature as the *unified postulate* because it is *the* unifying factor in the cosmos. All living things are generated and integrated through this pattern of wholeness. It is the one law that dictates the self-organization of energy and matter, from cosmology (the forces involving light, stars, orbits, and gravity), through biology (the forces of evolution), to human psychology (the forces of personal and social transformation).

When Jesus proclaimed a "second coming," he may have been alluding to a time when all people would clearly understand the pattern of wholeness, which the Qabalah has retained, hidden in the original symbols of the alphabet and the text of Genesis, awaiting our recognition of it.

The language of Qabalah consists of Autiot—its symbols—each of which has a cosmic meaning. For example, *Aleph*, the first Aut, is the intermittent spark of life that is ever recurring, though never the same. It is life, but not existence, because existence has duration and Aleph itself does not. Until we build a neural network in our brain that differentiates between life and existence, we will never understand the Aleph. It offers a perception voiced by Mel Gibson, playing the part of William Wallace in the film *Braveheart:* "Everyone dies. Not everyone lives."

Growing up in a culture and using the language of that culture shapes or frames the brain's perceptual maps, limiting our choices of interpretation to specific cultural biases, many having their roots in the limitations of the senses. Qabalah gives us another lens, a cosmic lens, by allowing us to perceive awareness through the activity of cosmic forces, the Autiot. This expands the brain's perceptual abilities beyond the limits of cultural perspectives, into the realm of the forces that actually created the brain, giving the brain a new perspective of its own nature.

In Genesis the Qabalists presented the pattern of wholeness in several ingenious ways throughout the text. The pattern can be recognized only (initially) if the text is studied letter by letter, because it is revealed through the code that positions the letters. The code is quite simple. All the words of text are actually acronyms. For instance, "the Lord" is the acronym YHWH, derived from the first letters of the names of the Autiot, Yod-Hay-Waw-Hay. Yod is a physical container, the body. Waw (or Vav) is the sixth Aut in the Qabalic system, a fertilizing agent. Hay, fifth Aut in the Qabalic system, is the archetype of life. YHWH has two Hays—one for inner life and the other for outer life. Therefore, YHWH is not a deity, but rather a reference to the continual process of inner life fertilizing outer life and outer life fertilizing inner life. It is the self-awareness and transformation that unfold as we process data from both our inner and outer worlds, naturally producing changes and alterations in behavior. YHWH is a process that can occur only in human beings, the simple process of recognizing when our actions fail to result in what we intended, producing a change in our behavior so that the desired intentions can then be realized. When YHWH is read linguistically, it becomes the clumsy "Yahweh," and irrevocably loses its original, sacred meaning. Its interpretation as the Lord, or Jehovah, is equally misleading.

Perhaps the code of Qabalah (acronymically, QBLH) originated with ancient shamans, but we may never know, just as we may never know why the earth spins. What we do know is that it provided the Autiot, which later became the symbols of the Hebrew alphabet. The Greek alphabet was adapted from the Hebrew, the Roman from the Greek, and the English from the Roman, all using the same twenty-seven symbols, which have been reduced in English by only one, leaving twenty-six. Throughout the sweeping cultural and linguistic changes of Western civilization, the original alphabet—its name derived from the first two Autiot of the code, Aleph and Bayt—has remained astonishingly intact, a testament to its unified source.

The Western alphabet is the most widely used alphabet in the world. Its fertility is a testament to the pattern of wholeness embedded in its original structure, the Qabalah. The study of Qabalah introduces the pattern of wholeness to the human brain and induces the brain to develop a new level of perception. The code in Genesis contains the knowledge of the interplay between opposites, delineating the forces that generate and animate everything: the universe and ourselves within it. We are familiar with this pattern in a seed, as germ and husk. As men and women this pattern is obvious in our genitals; male genitals are exterior to the body, while female genitals are interior. The pairing of body and soul provides another example of the inner/outer dynamic. In each pair, the two elements are complementary and mutually self-defining: One cannot exist without the other.

SACRED ALPHABET OF CREATION

The functioning of the universal pattern of wholeness in the structure of the Hebrew letters has been clarified by Stan Tenen, who has been working with the Hebrew alphabet for over twenty years, not from the standpoint of Qabalah, but by using his particular gift for pattern recognition. A year after having a moving experience at the Western Wall in Jerusalem, Tenen thought to examine the Hebrew Bible he had been given about ten years earlier. Because he couldn't read Hebrew, he simply looked at the text. Astonished, he could clearly see a pattern in the letters of the first verse of Genesis. It took him a few years to work out the pattern, but when he did he discovered that it revealed the significance of ancient geometries that represent successive steps in embryonic self-generation and self-organization, like the pattern of ontogeny recapitulating phylogeny.

Tenen's work demonstrates a deeper and previously unappreciated relationship between ancient and modern philosophical, scientific, and spiritual paradigms. His work brings to light many new and powerful insights concerning the nature of living systems, not only the cosmological system within which this planet resides and the biological/ecological systems of earth that gave rise to the human form, but also, most important for us, the neurological living system that exists within our own bodies—the brain and nervous system, from which all perception, consciousness, and awareness arise and then produce culture.

Tenen organized what he calls the Meru Project and began his research by building models of the mathematical structure he discovered in the letters, which he now refers to as the Geometric Metaphor. This mathematical structure and metaphor accurately represents the self-organizing attributes of living, whole systems and is a perfect model of duality-in-unity, the pattern of integrated opposites. "For thousands of years," states Tenen, "spiritual teachers of the Abrahamic traditions have claimed that the Hebrew symbols are 'holy' letters, descended directly from heaven, and that if studied with proper care, they will reveal the profoundest possible knowledge of life in the universe and the nature and purpose of human consciousness."*

Based on work accomplished so far, Tenen hypothesizes that the structure of the letters of the Hebrew alphabet—their shape and the method of their formation—was specifically created to illustrate the interplay between cosmology and human consciousness as an elegant, simple, and beautiful relationship of process. According to a Meru Foundation report, "Current linguistic and paleographic scholarship proposes that ancient phonetic alphabets developed from pictographic and hierarchical symbols,"† while certain religious teachings maintain that the Hebrew, Greek, and Islamic alphabets consist of "sacred" letters whose intrinsic geometric forms are an expression of creation as a whole-systems pattern.

Meru research has reconstructed details of geometries previously lost, demonstrating an organized and ordered basis for narratives in sacred texts (such as the Bible) that are often dismissed as poetic. This research demonstrates how the letters of the "sacred" alphabets of the Western tradition represent real, natural elements of the universe and, most important, of human consciousness. For example, Tenen discovered that when the underlying pattern of the first verse of Genesis is revealed geometrically, it forms the essential pattern that gives rise to the torus—a three-turn vortex wound on a doughnut, a figure that elegantly conveys the relationship between inner and outer. Every complex living whole system, according to Qabalah, is organized with the pattern of inner and outer. Time follows the same pattern, with the opposites of continuity and disruption. Continuity is the outer element, disruption is the inner.

The canonized Hebrew text of Genesis, letter for letter, has been faithfully reproduced exactly as it was originally. Not one letter has been replaced or removed, not one in three thousand years, because, as Stan Tenen reveals, the code is self-correcting. Tenen has discovered that

*Stan Tenen, *The Meru Project* (San Anselmo, Calif.: Meru Foundation, 1994).
†Stan Tenen, *The Meru Project*.

the entire Hebrew alphabet has properties somewhat similar to those of a hologram: It can be reconstructed from any part of itself, as well as from the whole of the first verse of Genesis. (More fascinating details of Meru geometric models and their relationship to the code of Qabalah can be found in appendix 2.)

GENESIS AND PERSONAL GROWTH

Few people could penetrate this ancient knowledge at the time it was written, but amazingly it has been preserved in Genesis intact.

We are now more prepared to perceive it the way it was intended, as an exercise for personal growth, capable of strengthening our inner powers of recognition, insight, and clarity so we can achieve the love, happiness, and wisdom we yearn for and that are the natural outcome of personal transformation and wholeness.

One major purpose of the code in Genesis is to bring us to the place where we truly understand the generative power inherent in words and symbols as tools for the evolution of the mind and, subsequently, of culture. This is a critical aspect of language. We are the creators of our words. We create their meanings and their meanings give rise to awareness and, subsequently, to culture. Therefore, we are the creators of our culture. When most of us think about our culture, however, we usually mistakenly assume that culture *is life*. Yet Qabalah makes clear that life is a whole-systems creation. Patriarchal culture, on the other hand, is not, because it diminishes the feminine component by assuming male authority. As Elaine Morgan pointed out in her hilarious commentary on paleoanthropology, *The Descent of Woman,* "A very high proportion of . . . thinking . . . is androcentric in the same way that pre-Copernican thinking was geocentric."* There are neural networks in our brains that now automatically produce patriarchal perspectives, which we assume are correct in the same way that the early church assumed the sun revolved around the earth, an assumption that led to the imprisonment

*Elaine Morgan, *The Descent of Woman* (New York: Stein and Day, 1972), 3.

of Galileo for daring to state otherwise. The only way to clear such distortions of patriarchy from our minds is to clean our linguistic house, to cease using the masculine identifying nouns *man* and *mankind* and the pronoun *he* in generalizations. These perspectives feed into our processes of self-definition. It's like walking a maze: If you make a wrong turn at the beginning, all subsequent turns will be wrong. So it is with language and self-definition. If a word promotes distortion, all subsequent definitions based on the original distortion will also be distorted. By using the language of wholeness, we support our search for authentic happiness. We are formed through a whole-systems dynamic. We can't discover meaning or happiness without first recognizing that basic fact and employing it in our linguistic self-definition processes.

Symbols carry a special fertility insofar as the growth of our neurology is concerned. Whatever the eye sees, whether outwardly or inwardly, becomes a symbol in the mind and is processed through special neurons and neural networks that exist in the visual processing centers of the brain. Although our eyes may gather the light, about 80 percent of all visual processing and interpretation is done by the brain. What most of us do not realize—what Genesis addresses, and Jesus afterward, and science now—is that our brain often processes information incorrectly yet unknowingly. Understanding how the mind processes symbols into information is one of the central purposes of this myth, especially the symbols *good* and *evil,* which, as we will see, have been interpreted exactly opposite their original meaning. As Bill so eloquently demonstrated, the mind can trick itself. Native Americans have a special mythological character for this mental trickery: Coyote Prankster. Bill had captured his Coyote Prankster by recognizing its trickery. How often are we fooled by the way the brain interprets information? In order to capture the Coyote Prankster at work, we must be aware and vigilant, watching closely how the brain processes information.

The brain must *learn* to frame the information inherent in symbols as clearly as possible. We must be able to *perceive* and *interpret* clearly the information we term *reality,* or we would not know that the sun does not cross the sky the way our eyes tell us it does, especially if we do not have a telescope and an insightful mind like Galileo's to reveal otherwise. Coyote Prankster is the brain's trickster, often deluding it into believing what the senses tell it even though that may not be the truth. Our job is to capture the mind's trickster through simple awareness. Coyote Prankster cannot operate if we see what he's doing.

The senses are often fooled about reality, especially when the subject is the behavior of light in human consciousness. If we wish to know the reality concerning light in ourselves, we must dig deep beneath the surface of the senses, deep into the brain's neural organization, examining its processes of interpretation. Incredibly, this is a world that is completely *non*sensory, and this is where Genesis takes us if we read it mythologically.

The code of Qabalah in Genesis reveals the process by which the alphabetic symbols of Western civilization are generated. It strips them of any and all cultural, phonetic, or linguistic associations, leaving only their essence, the Autiot. This stripping away of the cultural associations of alphabetic symbols is a potent function that allows the mind to reconstruct its perceptions of what reality is and who we are. The mind rebuilds its perceptions, stone by stone, reconstructing our house of awareness upon the solidity of truth that factually *is* reality—the whole-systems dynamic—instead of the sand of patriarchal illusion.

By building our perceptions upon the solid foundations of reality's whole systems, we learn to see deeply and clearly. We then become, as it were, new beings—not cultural beings but cosmic beings, because we understand that wholeness is universal.

COSMOLOGY AND MYTHOLOGY

After the pattern of recovering wholeness is recognized at the letter level in Genesis, it suddenly becomes apparent at other levels too, because the brain is now alert to the pattern. It appears in the two story lines at the beginning of Genesis—the creation story and the Garden of Eden story—one cosmological and the other mythological. The cosmology, narrating *outer* events, is told through the metaphor of the six days of creation in Genesis 1. The mythology, narrating *inner* events, is told through the metaphor of Adam and Eve in the Garden of Eden in Genesis 2, 3, and 4 (up to verse 16). This portion of the tale is the germ of the story, representing the inner life of the psyche.

The two story lines together reveal the pattern of wholeness as an integration of opposites—outer and inner—as the story moves from outer to inner. The cosmology and the mythology are beautifully intertwined in this ancient text. It's no wonder these words make up the first pages in the Bible, for they unmistakably present the pattern of integrated opposites. The pattern has been there all along, but who has recognized it? Fundamentalists have been so focused on the idea of creationism that the fact that Genesis narrates an evolutionary pattern seems to have escaped them altogether.

Cosmology, according to science, is an evolutionary process beginning with the Big Bang. The version Genesis tells in its first chapter, through the code of Qabalah, is as complex as the version science tells, especially now that quantum analysis has been added to the picture, with its elements of potentiality and possibility:

> *In the beginning God created the heaven and the earth.*
> *And the earth was without form, and void;*
> *and darkness was upon the face of the deep.*
> *And the spirit of God moved upon the face of the waters.*
> *And God said, Let there be light—*

Bang!

> *and there was light.*
> *And God saw the light, that it was good:*
> *and God divided the light from the darkness.*
> *And God called the light Day, and the darkness he called Night.*
> *And the evening and the morning were the first day.*

GENESIS 1:1–3

Qabalically, this narration of the first day is from the perspective of the first Aut, Aleph (see appendix 1), the spark of life that fertilizes every self-generative process. Likewise the second day is a narrative from the perspective of the second Aut, Bayt, the archetype of structure, or containers. It is a treatise on the interplay between energy and matter (the germ of life and its containers), the never-ending cycle of creation and destruction that yields new creation. All destruction carries with it the seeds of new life. Resurrection is always the natural outcome of death. The universe constantly builds containers, then destroys them, so that new containers can be built from the ashes of the old. Nature always uses the emissions of one system as fuel for another. The narration of this interplay between energy and matter continues throughout the text.

Joseph Campbell made an observation about the relationship between cosmology and mythology that coincides with Qabalic insight. He said that every fruitful myth contains an up-to-date cosmology. Certainly the fruitfulness of Genesis has never been in doubt. It has given rise to many of the world's alphabets and three of its major religions.

That fruitfulness, the Qabalists insisted, is rooted in the Principle of Indetermination, which recognizes that all whole systems self-generate in an indeterminate manner. Every seed has the potential to produce an indeterminate number of future plants, fruits, and seeds. It is the germ that contains this potential, this secret dowry.

All seeds, unless they are defective in some way, have the potential to produce more seeds. We know that. We also know, if we think about it, that the number of potential new plants and new seeds contained within any seed is indeterminate. We can never accurately count them because we do not know how many are yet in the future. Therefore, life is both a gigantic fact *and* a mystery. The mystery—the unknown element of life—is the realm of fertility. How many possible possibilities are there?

The role of the Qabalah in the human mind is to fertilize all the seeds of possibilities, inducing a state of indetermination. Each of us is a vast ocean of innate potential, like wet clay that can be formed into an infinite variety of shapes, then rolled back into a ball and reshaped and re-formed an infinite number of times. The pattern of indeterminate potential in a seed is present in our bodies when the germ of our childhood actualizes into the adult, who can continually become new through new realizations and insights, just as a tree can continually produce new fruit. The psyche, though it is invisible to our senses, transits through such phases. When a mature psyche is fruitful, insight produces a continual enlarging of awareness that *is* our indeterminate potential: "By their fruits shall they be known."

All of us contain within the neural networks of the brain this amazing indeterminate potential for growth. Neurons in the brain grow much like germs within seeds. They self-generate in an indeterminate manner. The Qabalists insisted that this quality of neural self-generation, scientifically defined as *neurogenesis,* is the foundation of human adaptability. It occurs, for example, when an apple falling from a tree (outer world) is suddenly seen (inner world) as the basis of a new law—gravity—which is merely a new *interpretation* of familiar events.

Seeing the pattern of cosmology and mythology in Genesis is, likewise, a new interpretation of a familiar story. It allows us to perceive, for instance, that layered within its carefully constructed verses is a scientific analysis in line with modern evolutionary evidence. That evidence is presented in the *pattern* of creation.

Light was created first, on the first day. Heaven (energy/potential) was created on the second day. Earth was created on the third day. During earth's creation, water came first, then dry land.

> *And God said, Let the waters under the Heaven*
> *be gathered together unto one place, and let the*
> *dry land appear: and it was so.*

> *And God called the dry land Earth;*
> *and the gathering together of water he called Seas . . .*
> GENESIS 1:9–10

Then terrestrial life on earth appeared, in a specific order. First came plants, then all the animals, beginning with those in the water (birds are more celestial than terrestrial), then those on land, moving through mammals, to hominids, and finally culminating with humans (on the sixth day). One detail is:

> *And the earth brought forth the grass and herb*
> *yielding seed after its kind, and the tree,*
> *yielding fruit whose seed is in itself . . .*
>
> GENESIS 1:12

This image, of a fruit whose seed is in itself, details the recursive action of life, how it builds containers, then destroys them so new containers can be built. If the fruit isn't eaten (destroyed), the seed remains in a dormant state. But if the fruit is eaten, seeds often withstand the digestive processes and are dropped on the ground in a new spot to begin the process all over again. This action of building containers, ever more complex—from plants, to animals, to mammals, to hominids— continues until finally a container emerges like no other.

In verse 26, humans first appear:

> *And God said, Let us make man [sic] in our image, after our likeness:*
> *and let them have dominion over the fish of the sea,*
> *and over the fowl of the air, and over the cattle,*
> *and over all the earth, and over every creeping thing*
> *that creepeth upon the earth.*
>
> GENESIS 1:26

A hidden element lies in the fact that verse 26 contains humanity's first appearance. The number 26 has deep significance. It is the number of YHWH, the so-called "Lord" (of Genesis IV). If you add up the numbers of the symbols Yod-Hay-Waw-Hay (refer to appendix 1), they equal 26. In other words, their appearance in verse 26, the number of

YHWH (Yod-Hay-Waw-Hay), is one indication that human beings contain the potentiality of YHWH, the Lord.

Paradoxically, another translation for YHWH is *loaf,* as in a loaf of bread. Bethlehem-Judah means "house of bread." This is where the reference of Jesus' body to bread originates.

How did the authors of Genesis, three thousand years ago, know that light was the first element in cosmic creation, that our planet was covered with water before land appeared, that life began with plants and only later produced animals, that those animals began in the water and evolved to those on land, and that they progressed in complexity from primitive creatures until human beings appeared?

The Genesis 1 vision of cosmology is nothing if not clear, distinct, and complete. It forms the husk of the myth, because it narrates *outer* events, right up to the sixth day, which even then reveals the potentiality of inner light, with humans first appearing in verse 26. The problem with rigid perceptions of the myth is that the inclusion of that process within a six-day period has been *assumed* to mean six literal days. If you understand the Qabalah, however, the number six has a very specific meaning; it is this Qabalic meaning that dictates the way the information in the story should be framed. The sixth Aut of the Qabalic system, Waw (or Vav), carries two meanings: the number 6 and the quality of fertility. Our word *sex* is derived from the Latin word for *six.* A structure with six angles is defined as *sexangular.* A *sexagenarian* is someone whose age is in the sixth decade. The creation of human beings on the sixth day, in verse 26, is meant to be understood in the context of fertility that Waw emits, which leads to the potential unfolding of YHWH, later in the story.

Without the Qabalic knowledge pertaining to the number 6, or the implications of the information in verse 26, the true depths of the meaning of this text are lost, and any number of assumptions can be used to interpret the myth, though they will all be erroneous, just as we all assumed my daughter was saying "up" to indicate my husband's head when what she was really trying to communicate is that his hat was on the top shelf of the closet. Coyote Prankster again.

THE SEVENTH DAY

One of the patterns seldom noticed in Genesis is that the seventh day begins a new chapter. This signifies that biological evolution—narrated in Genesis 1 as the six days of creation—is now over. After the cosmological narrative of *outer* events in Genesis 1 ends with the sixth day, Genesis 2 moves in the opposite direction, to an *inner* mythology. The seventh day begins a new evolution (a new chapter) of awareness within the human brain. Verses 1 through 4 of Genesis 2 orient to the seventh day, the last day of this story. Astonishingly, we are still living in this seventh day.

> *Thus the heavens and the earth were finished,*
> *and all the host of them.*
> *And . . . he rested on the seventh day*
> *from all his work which he had made.*
> *And God blessed the seventh day, and sanctified it.*
>
> GENESIS 2:1–3

The seventh day represents the freeing of our indeterminate potential, 7 being the Qabalic number of indetermination. Paradoxically, both the freeing and the restriction of that potential occur through human culture. The matter of the human brain was produced during the cycle of biological evolution narrated in Genesis 1. We now know, through science, that it was completed somewhere between 150,000 and 40,000 years ago with full expansion of the frontal lobes, giving our forehead its distinctive high-browed silhouette. Genesis 2 begins the story of the initiation of culture in the human brain through the processing of symbols. In other words, Genesis 2 does not continue the evolutionary (outer) story of Genesis 1. Rather, a *dis*continuity is introduced. Life changes direction, from matter to energy, from husk to germ, from outer to inner. In the last forty thousand years, the only changes in the human brain have been the ideas—the information—within it. The husk is represented by the matter of the brain, while the germ is the symbolic information being processed within it, thus fertilizing, flowering, and fruiting our awareness.

Culture is the final cycle in the saga that is the development of the human nervous system. The seventh-day cycle, the fertilizing, flowering, and fruiting of our full awareness, can occur only if the information in symbols is organized according to the reality of indeterminate potential, represented by Zayn, the seventh Aut of Qabalah (see appendix 1). We are still living in this seventh day, the day of Zayn.

The processing of symbols as information in the neural tissue of the brain is first evidenced by the startling and beautiful drawings on cave walls all over the world that date back thirty thousand to forty thousand years, and some scientists say even seventy thousand years. These first symbols were most likely produced by shamans. The importance of such imagery can't be overemphasized. It led to symbolic art and metaphorical storytelling, introducing the social element of our evolution.

Symbols both arise from and are processed within the human brain, in which the psyche is fully invested. By symbols I do not mean written symbols alone, but any type of symbol—including art, photographs, and imagery—because symbols provide the data that is processed as information. In fact, everything the eyes see becomes a symbol processed within the brain's neural structures. All symbolic information, then, must be processed through visual mechanisms—that is, inner light. Literacy, however, adds an altogether different dimension to symbolic information, a social dimension that is often hidden from our awareness.

Alphabetic symbols are the foundation of all advanced cultures. The delineation between so-called primitive cultures and so-called advanced cultures is literacy. Representative of this was *Time* magazine's choice of Johannes Gutenberg, inventor of the printing press, for its "Man of the Millennium." Our simple twenty-six-symbol alphabet enabled the flowering of an indeterminate number of letter combinations to produce words, which express ideas. It also provided the masses with access to those ideas by being readily adaptable for use on a printing press, making the mass production of books possible for the first time in the history of Western culture, with the first book produced being the Bible.

However, there is a hidden relationship between literacy and social organization, as Leonard Shlain warns in *The Alphabet Versus the Goddess: The Conflict Between Word and Image* (Viking, 1998). The rise of literacy—a process that takes place almost exclusively in the (masculine) left hemisphere of the brain—also gave rise to powerful social cycles of misogyny. All over the world, Shlain points out, women's power was systematically destroyed by men as they gained the power of literacy. In China, foot binding reached its zenith a hundred years after the printing press was invented there, with the same material—linen—being used to bind women's feet and to produce manuscripts. Contrast that with the end of the so-called Dark Ages—a time of widespread illiteracy. Troubadours were singing the praises of women and knights pledged to protect them at all cost. Interestingly, after widespread literacy was introduced in the West with the rise of the printing press, witch hunts soon followed.

The influence of literacy on misogyny was further exacerbated by the concept of patriarchal monotheism, which *assumes* that God is both male and exterior to ourselves. The androcentric, compartmentalized packaging of information that monotheism creates is directly related—I believe along with Shlain—to the way the left hemisphere processes literate information *in isolation,* that is, without input from the right hemisphere and in a sequential manner.

Sitting alone (in a church, synagogue, or mosque) and reading words on a page in a sequential manner has a profound impact on the brain. Shlain proposes that it is the *process* of reading, rather than the meaning of words, that has such enormous influence on the way the brain interprets written information. That process, he asserts, results in an autocratic, misogynist intellect that assumes itself to be the sole arbiter of truth.

While there have always been sensitive, feminist, pluralist intellects in the world, the authorities of patriarchy have focused on masculine priorities: the territorialization of power and resources. We can see the results of such perceptions glaring at us from fundamentalist thought everywhere, which maintains the most rigid forms of interpretation of the scriptures while it also devalues and dominates women—and distracts our attention from inner awareness. This tendency of the monotheistically literate left hemisphere to dominate information processing while it dominates women underlies interpretations of the Genesis myth that view Eve as the original sinner, tempting Adam instead of saving him, preventing us all from understanding the true depths of this story.

What many of us fail to consider is that culture is self-defined and self-determined. *We* are the ones creating and interpreting *all* the symbols we use in our stories, including all the patriarchal, monotheistic, and misogynist paradigms. Oddly, we seem, for the most part, largely unaware of the power and influence we wield in this realm. Coyote Prankster plays with our mind, but remains hidden.

Qabalah is a system of knowledge that can be grasped only by the right hemisphere because its information is so complex it cannot be laid out or recognized in a linear, sequential manner. The right hemisphere processes data in an all-at-once gestalt. Unburdened by the sequencing of linear thought, it can grasp complexities the left hemisphere is utterly incapable of comprehending, such as whole-systems organization. I believe that the original teaching of the Qabalah—which had no association to phonetic or linguistic elements—somehow shifted into the phonetic system we know today as the alphabet, losing its original container of meaning—the indeterminate fertility of life—in the process. To this day Hebrew is written right to left, perhaps a shadowy vestige of its right-hemisphere Qabalic origins. Carlo Suares spent forty years in painstaking research to re-create it.

The seventh day—the symbolic day of Zayn inside the human psyche—represents the potential fertility involved in symbol processing (which is information processing) in the brain. At this point in culture, the seventh day has produced a brain that can process information through alphabetic symbols, but also a psyche that is tragically incomplete due to the patriarchal container of its symbols, which must give way to a new container of thought: whole systems. This new whole-systems container will grow inside our awareness as we process the information of wholeness through its symbols.

This new container of awareness is Qabalically revealed in Genesis in the evolution of the deity's name from Genesis 1 to Genesis 4. In Genesis 1, the name of the deity is God, or ELHYM (the Qabalic spelling). But in Genesis 2, the name of the deity changes to Lord God, or YHWH ELHYM. Traditional interpretations insist that the two names are still the one God, that for some reason God has many names, all meaning "God."

According to the Qabalah, however, the two names signify completely different processes. ELHYM points to the (outer) cosmological and biological processes of evolution, while YHWH is purely psychological (inner). Using the Autiot, we can see that ELHYM is Aleph-Lammed-Hay-Yod-Mem (1.30.5.10.40). According to the code of Qabalah, this sequence expresses the fact that the timeless discontinuous pulsations of Aleph (1) underlie the functional movement of organisms (30), their life (5), and all individual existences (10) with their resistance to destruction (40). This process can put into motion only the repetitive production of prototypes, ergo the evolution of species, until the "blessing" and "sanctifying" of number 7 (the seventh day, on which God blessed and sanctified, according to Genesis 2:3), which opens the way to all indeterminate possibilities in one species: human beings. The two processes (outer and inner) are intertwined in the literate brain, which can now study the processes of evolution and ponder them. YHWH ELHYM, an amalgamation of the two processes, is therefore the deity in Genesis 2, which begins the narrative of the inner journey to full awareness. All this is lost in traditional interpretations, however, in which monotheism still reigns supreme and where there is no recognition of the difference between God and the Lord God, between ELHYM and YHWH ELHYM.

As for the name of the deity, it changes once more, in Genesis 4, to simply YHWH—a new awareness based on whole systems. The Autiot in the name YHWH define the pattern of wholeness in human beings, which will be clarified as we move along.

The pattern of whole systems is such that husks are created first, then the power of germs is awakened within. Literacy is a husk, a container, which has produced a static, rigid, authoritarian intellect interested more in domination than in integration. As we awaken to the power of intention, invested in the frontal lobes (represented by Eve in Genesis), the static, rigid mind of patriarchy will give way to the flowering of new cultural and psychological organization.

The power of intention is fertilized by insight, a *disruptive* energy emitted by the first Aut of the Qabalah, Aleph. When Aleph is witnessed, when the spark of inner light appears and is recognized (Aha!), suddenly the brain's continuity (the continuity of its cultural biases and rigidities) is disrupted. New energy rushes in, shifting our focus, which is precisely what happens in Genesis as the story moves from outer to inner, from Genesis 1 to Genesis 2.

Genesis shows us the ingredients involved in the construction of our internal maps of perception and symbolic information-processing mechanisms. By becoming aware of our brain's structure and processes, we can learn to recognize those static ideas and paradigms, such as good and evil, holding us hostage to crippling social patterns that will never produce anything but misery and suffering. Once we have recognized the true pattern of wholeness, we are able to break out of our self-imposed containers of thought.

The Garden:
Landscape of the Brain

As I was driving her to kindergarten one day, my oldest daughter asked, "Mommy, where does God live?" I thought about it for a minute, then replied, "In your heart." A few years later she asked, "Why is the sky blue?" And, "What holds up the clouds?" Contrast those with the questions my middle daughter asked. Her first was, "How are roads made?" Her second was, "How is bread made?" She continued to ask questions about how things are made and never once asked about God, the sky, or clouds. Different brains process information differently. My oldest daughter now studies math, science, and art. My middle daughter is an athlete.

I've always been fascinated by how we process information and what effect cultural paradigms have upon the brain's functions. What I've learned is that culture and language exert enormous influence over the brain's information-processing mechanisms. The influence of language patterns can be seen in the development of a child's brain. Up until the age of six months, a baby's brain is so attuned to different sounds that it can hear and process any sound that a human being can make. But after six months, the baby's brain begins to zero in on only the particular sounds in the languages that are repeatedly spoken in its presence. A baby exposed to many languages will continue to process all the sounds of those multiple languages. But a baby repeatedly exposed to only one language will begin to prune its auditory reception more finely until the only sounds its brain processes linguistically are the sounds of the one language spoken in its presence. So it goes with culture. The brains of babies born into a culture will process the information present in that culture, including all its inherent social patterns.

A DIFFERENT STRESS RESPONSE

Social patterns deeply influence two specific activities that are fundamental to human psychological and social organization: stress and affection. Shelley E. Taylor, a psychologist and stress researcher at UCLA, in her new book, *The Tending Instinct: How Nurturing Is Essential to Who We Are and How We Live* (New York: Times, 2002), points out that women have a much different stress response from men. The "fight or flight" response, assumed to be universal, is not. Women have completely different stress neurochemicals, which induce them to act differently from men under stressful conditions. What Taylor and her colleagues discovered was that more than 90 percent of all stress research was done on males, which is how the "fight or flight" response was discovered and named. But Taylor has now upset that applecart. Women's stress response has been dubbed "the tend and befriend" pattern because women under stress tend to children and befriend other women. This tending, nurturing activity provided by women turns out to be a major factor in the evolution of our intelligence and spirituality, and in our basic human nature. Taylor relates that as the day-to-day survival needs of hunter-gatherers transformed into the needs of a population of settled agriculturalists, the deeper significance of group life became clearer. Cooperative tasks of hunting and warfare are the least of what the social group can accomplish. Group living is intrinsically soothing and comforting. We enjoy not only a happier life but also a longer life in social groups because they promote growth and health through nourishing relationships. Of course, we are the source of one another's stress as well. But Taylor points out that nurturing behavior, especially affection, is more powerful even than nutritional supplements in promoting growth, both in awareness and in physiology.

One study she cites, carried out in Germany after WWII, proved that war orphans who received affection and nurturing grew faster and became healthier than those who lived with strict, emotionally distant caregivers, even thogh the latter received nutritional supplements.*

Taylor provides overwhelming evidence that we are basically a nurturing species. Our brain and body are crafted to tend to others (not indiscriminately) in order to attract, maintain, and nurture relationships across the life span. There is even a special neurophysiology, *affiliative neurocircuitry,* that mediates this nurturant behavior, which, when active, softens the chemicals of stress. Throughout her book, Taylor recalls study after study promoting the value of women's nurturant attention on their children, friends, and spouses as major contributions to societal cohesiveness. Through all the wars, famines, droughts, economic downturns, governmental abuses, and atrocities (such as slavery), women have kept society growing in awareness by activating our affiliative neurocircuitry. Stress, as we all know, can lead to disease, and disease to death. So affection is life-giving energy. Affection keeps us healthy, happy, and smart.

In contrast, patriarchy devalues affection; authorities tend to use punishment to maintain control. Pain is the guardian of patriarchy. A patriarchal man is a tough guy, unemotional and rational, making hard decisions for survival. But we aren't merely surviving anymore. We have now become so numerous that our population alone threatens to unbalance nature. What we need now is a new organization for society, which can only come about through new awareness, a new way of seeing.

---

*Shelley E. Taylor, *The Tending Instinct: How Nurturing Is Essential to Who We Are and How We Live* (New York: Times Books, 2002), 8.

One of the major ways that stress affects our social world is through violence, most of it exhibited by men. In our everyday lives, much of that violence has been watered down to what we commonly refer to as discipline, which often amounts to punishment instead, and to a lack of simple affection. Discipline is a necessary ingredient of wholeness. We can't be whole without discipline. But punishment is pain administered by one person to another, often rationalized as discipline to make it seem necessary. Punishment cannot be delivered unless one person has more power than another, or unless one person is perceived as having more power than another: parents who have more power than children, the state that has more power than the captured criminal or the common citizen. Punishment often goes hand in hand with a lack of affection. One study suggests that the memory impairments commonly associated with old age may have their roots in early-childhood affection deprivation, because memory is affected by hormones and stress. Our inner world, the organization of our neural networks, is deeply affected by its outer environment, especially its outer social environment, in which patriarchy and its authoritarian guardians use pain, or the threat of pain through punishment, to control not only people's behavior, but also their thoughts and feelings, causing a general rigidity of the mind.

While much has been written about the social and political ramifications of patriarchy, not much has been written about its psychological and spiritual effects. Qabalah is concerned with the psychological and spiritual influences that patriarchy exerts on the brain, making it rigid and static, because a static mind prevents flexibility and fertility of thought, diminishing inner awareness. The dissolving of that rigidity is at the core of the Genesis mythology because the aim of Qabalah is to generate in the mind of its students the most flexible intellectual state possible.

The disruption of rigid minds and rigid social institutions is at the heart of Qabalic thought and practice because disruption is a way of introducing life back into systems that have become dead, rigid, and inflexible. Not coincidentally, rigid minds resist disruption. Disruption is what revolution is all about. It is the force through which this country was born. It is the force that ended slavery. It is the force behind the decade of the 1960s, with its civil rights protests and marches. Disruption is a vital part of democracy *and* the life of the psyche.

Disruption is the shattering of a container that has become too small, like the eggshell of an emerging chick, the cocoon of a new butterfly, or the patriarchy that deadens our spirit. In us, in the psyche, such containers may be rigid religious beliefs or false ways of thinking; they may be illusions we have about others or ourselves that confine us to ways of living and behaving that depress the soul. Disruption is needed to open these containers that have become too small for our growing awareness. Containers, by the way, are designed to be shattered. That is their nature: temporary protection. If they were not designed this way, every chick would die in its shell, every butterfly would wither in its cocoon.

The universe is perpetually constructing and shattering containers. Qabalah and its mythology teach us to become aware of this process so we can integrate that knowledge into our awareness. Our job is to allow that process to occur within us, psychologically, so that our mind stays flexible, open, and perceptive, like the proverbial fountain of youth.

RECOGNITION AND GROWTH

Einstein once said that no problem can be solved from the consciousness that created it. We cannot understand wholeness from a consciousness of incompleteness. What we need in order to solve the problems of incompleteness is the knowledge of wholeness. Qabalah offers that knowledge through the code embedded in Genesis, but in order for us to access that knowledge, we must first *recognize* it.

The word *recognize* originates from the Latin *recognoscere*. *Re* means "again" and *gnoscere* is "to learn." (*Gnostic* is "to know.") *Recognize* has many meanings. Literally, it is "to learn, or know, again." Within that knowing and learning are many elements: "to identify, to acknowledge, to be aware of, and to take notice of"—all skills related to perception and activated through indwelling light.

Recognition is the psyche's germ power generating the construction of neural seedlings, which will then grow into networks that provide interpretation. It is far more useful in regaining wholeness than is affirmation, hope, prayer, or meditation. Recognizing the relationship between opposites that creates the pattern of wholeness is like harnessing to a locomotive the soul's internal journey of growth. Meditation, hope, prayer, and affirmation are ways to focus attention inward, so that recognition can take place. But recognition is the muscle of inner growth.

The pattern of wholeness is a universal constant and creates in the mind that understands it an awareness of cosmic organization. Such a mind leaps the boundaries of cultural perspective and begins to understand the nature of the cosmos. Such knowledge is neither humanly nor culturally based. It is a *recognition* of cosmic pattern. That recognition has been termed *transcendence*.

Everyone is capable of experiencing it, for it is the element that integrates us within cosmic life. No other person's transcendent experience, not even Jesus,' can substitute for one's own, because transcendence provides the authenticity upon which the psyche builds its character. Religion often seeks to substitute our personal experience of transcendence with the mandates of external authorities. But such a pattern will never help humanity. It will only keep humanity handcuffed in illusory beliefs.

Qabalah, if studied with intention, will eventually produce that recognition and transcendence. It is an instruction manual that teaches the brain to see the hidden relationships in wholeness and how they fit together. The primary relationship is between universal opposites, *inner* and *outer*—hence, we have an *inner life* and an *outer existence*.

To the Qabalists this distinction is fundamental. Inner *life* is of the psyche wherein we develop our spiritual and psychological awareness through the growth of neural networks in the brain. This is the feminine half of the equation. Outer *existence* is composed of the body's behavior in the world, the masculine half of the equation. Inner life is *active;* it grows as a germ grows. Outer existence is *static,* like a husk, because it does not grow except by means of inner awareness.

Among all of earth's creatures, humans have the greatest potential for change because we have the most germ power invested in our brains. If the interplay between awareness and behavior is allowed to develop authentically, it will naturally lead to self-growth and maturity. Too often, because our culture is built on the foundation of outer authority, inner awareness is not allowed into the feedback system. Therefore we have created a social system in which external forces—social values, attitudes, and laws—are relied on to dictate the course of culture. In such societies, humans are left incomplete, without the knowledge of either wholeness or its application to human personal and social endeavors.

THE MYTHOLOGICAL JOURNEY TO HAPPINESS

Inner life is like a hero's journey. According to Joseph Campbell, the hero's journey is a classic pattern of myth. It is a metaphor that describes a necessary struggle if we wish to revitalize the parts of our wholeness that have been repressed by patriarchal practices and attitudes. This is why it is a *hero's* journey: Heroes are those who engage in the battle, who fight the fight, who search for the mythological valued object, the Holy Grail, the magic elixir. Most of us are familiar with the hero-rescues-damsel-in-distress theme. Few of us recognize, however, that it is true psychologically. The hero's journey is a discovery and cherishing of inner (feminine) territory, the soul itself, its wholeness and beauty.

Every psyche contains masculine and feminine elements and they must be integrated if we wish to function as whole human beings, the only way of functioning that produces happiness. In the novel *Stranger in a Strange Land,* by Robert Heinlein (New York: Putnam, 1961), Michael Valentine Smith, an archetype of the Christ in the novel, states:

"Happiness is functioning the way a being is designed to function." We are designed to function with a whole psyche. If we wish to be whole, we must develop and integrate the feminine with the masculine. If we do not become the hero in our own life and recover our own wholeness, we can never be happy, no matter how much comfort, wealth, power, status, fame, or authority we may acquire.

There is no substitute for wholeness. None. Wholeness is the missing element in our culture's academic institutions, whether they are religious or secular, which is why the quest for the knowledge of wholeness is dependent upon investigations by lonely heroes who toil outside established institutions.

The mythology of the Garden of Eden portion of the text of Genesis reveals a classic hero's journey being undertaken by the human brain in order to retrieve the elixir that is the knowledge of wholeness. The hero represents the transformation of patriarchal mentality by rescuing and restoring the value of the inner realm, the feminine indwelling light, thereby restoring balance to the two opposites. It is a journey of integration and clarity as the brain seeks to actively grow, from its feminine germ of indeterminate potential, the neural networks that provide an awareness of its various parts and how they fit together in order to know its own wholeness, in which the psyche finds healing and joy.

Qabalah states that the journey to wholeness is not through external means, but by internal means, by recognizing and growing the powers of insight, awareness, and recognition in the brain and psyche, which is why the Genesis story revolves around an *eye-opening* event that has nothing to do with the physical sense of sight. Insight is an activity of germ energy within the human psyche, helping us to expand awareness, develop autonomy, and realize wholeness through neural growth and fecundity.

The simplest, most solid truth about being human is also the one absolute solid truth about life. It is this: All life, including the life of the human psyche, is a process of growth. Life equals growth. If something is alive, it is growing. If it is alive and growing, it is flexible. When it dies, rigidity and brittleness set in. *Rigor mortis* is a term we use to define the rigid quality of a corpse. But a mind in isolation, alone with its unchallenged thoughts, can be dead—rigid, inflexible, and brittle. Jesus said, "Let the dead bury their dead." (Luke 9:60)

When we are engaged in personal growth, we are in tune with life and we feel it because we regain our flexibility. When we recognize this, we do not need others—so-called experts and authorities, whether they be religious, psychological, or academic—to tell us how to manage our life, for one simple reason: All growth is self-generating and self-organizing. No amount of expert advice can help you achieve self-growth. You germinate it through the self-discovery of inner light and in this way undertake the genesis of your own personal transformation. A good therapist, insightful member of the clergy, or anyone familiar with the inner world can often help guide you through this process. But you are responsible for your own initiation, through intention, and your own growth, through awareness.

Because growth is the quality of life, green is its symbolic color, for green is the color of the plant life we see growing profusely all around us. When Moses talks to a burning bush that does not consume itself, the mythological image is one of a plant that is "burning" with the fire of life. The plant's life factually originates in the fire from the sun and is chemically processed through photosynthesis.

The Green Flame of Islam is a similar image. In the arid desert, green denotes the difference between life and death. Green became one of the colors of Muhammad, and is present on all Islamic flags. Western civilization would not have emerged had agriculture not first been adopted in the Fertile Crescent. Our agricultural heritage generated through the human ability to *see* the potential offered by cultivating seeds. Because this potential guaranteed us a food source, we settled down and began the task we are engaged in to this day, reorganizing our social interactions. Our agricultural heritage is embedded in our language and imagery and certainly in this myth, through the garden metaphor.

A seed needs no instruction in order to generate its innate potential, which is to grow into a plant that flowers and then fruits, producing new seeds containing new potential. And the cycle continues, each after its kind. The remarkable potential contained within every seed is hidden in its interior germ. The word *genesis* refers to this power, the power of self-*gen*eration, of growth—the power of the feminine.

The human psyche behaves like a seed in this sense. It too grows according to the universal pattern of life—that is, it self-generates in a garden of awareness. Like the seed, our personal growth is determined by the self-germination of inner potential. This inner potential, to a large extent, is contained in our ability to *see* in new ways. Inner seeing is the power behind discovering new possibilities, new technologies, and new ways of interacting with one another. As Jesus says in Luke 17:21, ". . . the kingdom of God is *within* you."

When Dorothy returns from Oz, she has an amazing story to tell. But no less amazing is her own realization and the growth in understanding it fosters. Though Dorothy's appears to be a magical tale full of fantastic creatures and unearthly scenery, on the psychological level it is basic truth, a story of personal growth and self-discovery. During her wild adventure, Dorothy learns to see that home is where the most valuable and important people and pieces of our life are, and she learns to recognize the value of real intellect, heart, and courage and to help others to recognize these in themselves.

These, then—personal growth and self-discovery—are the psyche's passions. Story is their medium and mythology is those stories. Dorothy's and Cinderella's and Adam and Eve's are stories the psyche weaves from its self-discovery and personal growth. This is what we can trust—our own growth—because we can mark its progress in wisdom gained, happiness recovered, and clarity achieved.

The deepest message of mythology is about personal transformation, about self-completion and wholeness, which can manifest in us only as we become aware of the power of indwelling light. This message offers the full shape of human potential, voicing our hopes and igniting our dreams for meaning and connection between women and men, sexuality and spirituality, humans and the environment and the divine.

ARCHETYPES FOR INTEGRATION

The purpose of the hero's journey to wholeness is to integrate the brain, because incompleteness forces the brain to become fragmented and compartmentalized. Integration is produced primarily through pattern recognition. Insight is the tool we use to recognize a pattern of previously hidden relationships, especially the interplay between inner awareness and outer behavior.

All the images of people, places, and things in this story are archetypes. Eve and Adam represent the two opposites of psyche (inner) and behavior (outer), respectively. Mythologically and Qabalically, the masculine outer element functions as a protective, contracting, and static husk. The feminine inner element functions as an active expanding germ. Beginning with Genesis 2:5, the story plunges into the interior of the human psyche and follows the classic pattern of a hero's journey. During this narrative it defines and describes human psychological development, using the image of a garden as an archetype of the interior landscape of the brain. This archetype functions at a number of levels simultaneously. A garden is where seeds grow. Our garden of awareness inside the brain is where the seeds of ideas, insight, and neurons grow. As we continue the journey through Genesis we will see how the elements of our neurological landscape are depicted through the garden metaphor; we will discover that familiar elements of the Genesis mythology, such as the relationship the man has to the garden and the trees, reveal precise arrangements of neurological factors now supported by scientific research.

A garden is a place for the practice of *agriculture,* defined by Webster's as "the science, art, or practice of cultivating the soil, producing crops, and raising livestock." The word *culture* is derived from *agriculture,* mirroring the development of culture from agriculture in human evolution. Agriculture leads to culture by producing enough surplus food to allow people to settle together in large numbers and create civilizations. Just as seeds represent the culturing of food as the body's fuel for growth, the garden is a fitting representation of the culturing of ideas through symbol processing as society's fuel for growth in awareness.

Agriculture was the first major process in which humans engaged in reorganizing their environment for themselves. That reorganizing of nature gave humans their first glimpse of the power of their own potential. The processing of cultural symbols in the human brain began, systematically, through the alphabet. Agriculture led to culture, which led to alphabetic-symbol processing, which led to the story of Genesis. The entire history of Western civilization can be summed up as that of a human cultural group acquiring the ability to process information using the symbols of the Western alphabet.

The linguistic intellect of the human brain separates us from all other animal species. We're different, no matter how many chromosomes we have inherited from chimpanzees. Linguistics makes our brain much more fertile with possibilities. This is the supreme message of the Qabalah: to maximize the fertility of possibility, just as the seed of every fruit maximizes its potential fertility. In this seventh day, the cycle of alphabetic-symbol processing in the human brain produces information and drives both cultural *and* neural evolution: our outer and inner worlds.

Beginning with agriculture, cultural forces have to a large degree replaced the forces of nature in training our brains to respond to their environment. Therefore *we* are now the major element that impacts our brain and its awareness, not God and not nature. It is time we recognize this fact and begin to attribute to ourselves that which we habitually attribute to God, nature, or evolution. It is the human social environment that now shapes the brain. And it is that social environment—patriarchal, monotheistic, and misogynist—that affects the psyche, leading to rigidity, incompleteness, and alienation. But the journey in

Genesis opens the way for disruptive energies to rejuvenate the psyche, inspiring awareness with creativity, flexibility, integration, and joy.

At the commencement of this journey to wholeness, in Genesis 2:5, a nameless man is introduced, along with his vocation. Naming is a significant event in Qabalic narrative because it stimulates intellectual growth. But attention must be paid to the circumstances in which it occurs or doesn't occur, as the case may be.

> *And every plant of the field before it*
> *was in the earth, and every herb of*
> *the field before it grew: for the Lord*
> *God had not caused it to rain upon the earth,*
> *and there was not a man to*
> *till the ground.*
>
> GENESIS 2:5

In order to engage the recognition processes of the brain, we must be aware that there are two things happening in this verse.

First, an introduction precedes actual events. The plants and herbs that do not yet exist are present in the verse, and therefore in our minds, because the authors are setting us up for possibilities waiting to happen that occur through a *pattern of relationships:* single acts that, added together, form a long chain of events integrated within a whole system. Second, the order of those events is opposite the order of events narrated in Genesis 1. The man is here created *first* instead of last, signifying that he is now positioned at the *beginning* of the process of psychological integration rather than at the *end* of the process of biological evolution narrated in Genesis 1.

Qabalah is saying that events are always preceded by other introductory events, like courses requiring prerequisites. This is a specific Qabalic technique used to reveal the significance of relationship in whole systems. Every act is preceded by a long chain of events. Nothing is compartmentalized, fragmented, or alienated. All events must be perceived within a whole-systems perspective. When we do not perceive the pattern of that long chain of events as being determined by relationship, our minds become compartmentalized and incapable of perceiving the truth of wholeness.

It is important to recognize that Genesis is *not* one continuous story. Rather, it is two stories in one, representing discontinuity within wholeness. Its discontinuity reveals the interplay between opposites—outer bodily existence and inner psychological life—that are always discontinuous yet always integrated. Outer physical chronology is much different from inner psychological chronology, yet they form a basic interplay that provides the fuel for growth in awareness when fully understood. Genesis 1 began with the creation of light and culminated with the creation of human beings: outer existence. Genesis 2 reveals, mythologically, the inner world of human consciousness and how inner light functions within it to expand awareness. This inner world is universal.

Adam's role is pivotal in this inner world, now rendered static by patriarchy and its authoritarian mind-set. He sits at the balancing fulcrum of psychological process, but he doesn't know that yet and neither do most of us. In order for Adam to fulfill his critical role in psychological development, he must recognize and integrate his opposite, the feminine. To accomplish that he must reevaluate how he has perceived her through the static lens of patriarchy. Finally, he must break the habit of thinking of himself as superior to her, as he must break the habit of thinking that any type of social hierarchy has validity in human societies. Hierarchy is a characteristic of animal societies that must not be mistaken for an appropriate human pattern.

The first important piece of information stated regarding Adam's role in Genesis 2:5 is not his name—his identity (which is so important in the patriarchal world)—but his vocation, which is to "till the ground." This is another of those subtle Qabalic messages; it reminds us that title, linked to the promotion of social hierarchy, is not important. Activity is what's important because our activities produce our fruits.

In traditional interpretations the importance of the archetypal ground in Genesis 2 has been almost entirely overlooked, but a closer examination reveals the introduction of a surprising element. The ground to be tilled is not only critical to the man's development but is also a theme that runs throughout the story. In the next verse we learn that the ground he is to till is the very dust from which he is created. What a curious riddle. The clue to its symbolic meaning is contained in the origin of the word *ground* itself. *Ground* in Hebrew is *adamah,* the feminine form of the word *Adam.* This feminine ground emerges before Adam, and Adam is created from it, through the long chain of events.

> *But there went up a mist from the earth*
> *and watered the whole face of the ground [Adamah].*

> *And the Lord God formed man of the*
> *dust of the ground [Adamah] and breathed into his*
> *nostrils the breath of life; and man*
> *became a living soul.*

> GENESIS 2:6–7

The Lord God, an amalgamated name, signifies the two energies now shaping the psyche: the matter that evolved during biological evolution and the neural patterns arising within that matter. The matter is referred to as Adamah, the ground of being. From this neural matter arise all the other elements in the myth: the man created from its dust, the trees, and the animals he later names. But first the matter must be fertilized.

This takes place in verse 6, the Qabalic number of fertilization. In this verse the acronymic formulas demonstrate a link between the rain and the ground: the rain is AD (Aleph-Dallet) and the ground is Adamah, ADMH (Aleph-Dallet-Mem-Hay). The acronyms for rain and ground both begin with AD, Aleph-Dallet, the spark of life and a resistance. Aleph (the first Aut), the supreme disruptive element, is now immersed in the nonresistant earth, from which the mist rises. *Earth* is a reference to the matter of the brain because it is the container of awareness. The mist that springs forth represents a resistance that does not belong to the limited response of the container. It is insight, belonging to Aleph. Its waters fertilize that earth, or container, transfiguring it in such a fashion as to give it the status of Adamah (ground). The earth becomes fertile ground. Mythologically, this verse is the depiction of the brain having the capacity to continually self-generate new neurons. All of this is lost in the linguistic translation, in which the ground is not recognized as the neural "ground of being and awareness" from which spiritual awakening occurs.

The act we are currently investigating, viewed Qabalically, signifies the fertilizing of our immense potential. That potential is a feminine, gestative, *neural* womb that generates symbols and all understanding of them, and of ourselves as creators of them. The substance of Adamah is the soil of the garden, which must be *actively* tilled if we wish to be fully aware. Tilling the ground is a metaphor for our active participation in the processes of awareness and its expansion through neurogeresis.

Here, Adam was created to till her but never actually does. Several times throughout this narrative Adam is ordered to till the ground or he is punished for not doing so, or is even punished by doing so. Yet Cain—designated a "tiller of the ground"—is the only one who actually accomplishes this task of transcendence (in Genesis 4:2), one of the clues that paints him a hero-son in this story, redeeming the villainous image he has been maligned with by traditional interpretations.

The actual substance from which Adam is formed is dust, symbolic of rocklike rigidity that has crumbled. Adam's substance is derived from the breaking of the rigid, repetitive patterns of the animals in our evolutionary heritage. It means that we humans, though produced by evolution, are nevertheless mostly free of evolution's instinctuality and rigidity, which is why human babies are so helpless at birth. We must be taught everything, which is culture's responsibility as the village that is needed to raise every child. Yet our culture is incomplete and produces incompleteness in us. We need to overcome our incomplete cultural biases and assumptions by interpreting this story in a new way.

ADAM IN THE GARDEN

And the Lord God planted a garden
eastward in Eden; and there he put the
man whom he had formed.

GENESIS 2:8

When the garden is introduced, it is important to note its place-ment in the east, for it is another of the overlooked yet significant themes in the story. As we will see later, east is where the tree of life is located. This direction for the placement of both the tree of life and the garden is another Qabalic clue revealing the nature of wholeness. It establishes the garden's character. East—where the sun rises—represents all the indeterminate potential present within human awareness, whether or not that potential is recognized or actualized. The sun ris-ing every day is an analogy for the new possibilities present in every new day. It is a metaphor revealing that the existence of new poten-tial—new life—is always present within us as disruptive energy, insti-gated by Aleph and signified by the *A* in AD and ADMH (Adamah). How we tap into that potential or even if we tap into it is determined by our recognition of it. Do we see it? Are we tilling this ground?

Qabalically, the garden of Eden is the exact opposite of what we have assumed it to be. It is incredibly volatile because the energy within the garden is ruled by the Aleph in Ayn. Ayn is the first Aut in the word *Eden.* It's a bit confusing because we spell Eden with an *E,* when *A* (Ayn) is the first Aut. Because the number of this disruptive element, Ayn, is 70 (see appendix 1), it is meant to shatter any continuum (meaning "fixation") that has become static and rigid, like a sacred cow. The life to which Adam is called is a series of destructions and reconstructions meant to keep him in a perpetual state of change and evolution. If Adam were to find any comfortable stability, he might settle down to become a lazy, sub-human species. In order to prevent that, he is deposited into an incredibly unstable neural environment, the Gan-Eden, or Garden of Eden, which is in constant upheaval, forever striving for every possible possibility of becoming. The peaceful, bucolic garden that we are accustomed to is a mirage. It has never existed, just as the earth has never been flat. Gan-Eden, the Garden of Eden, is the most explosively gestative neural state possible.

> *And out of Adamah made the Lord God*
> *to grow every tree that is pleasant to the*
> *sight, and good for food; the tree of life*
> *also in the midst of the garden, and the*
> *tree of the knowledge of good and evil.*
>
> GENESIS 2:9

With verse 9 we now have the major elements of the story so far: the man, the ground, the garden in the east, and those famous trees, which are particularly described as being "pleasant to the sight," an obvious reference to perceptual activities. With some rudimentary knowledge of the brain, these images can now be seen as neurological and psychological components in the brain and psyche.

The ground, as Adamah, is the actual tissue of the brain. She is the feminine womb that generates everything else in the story because she produces not only Adam (from whom Eve later emerges), but also the famous trees and other animals he will name in verses 2:19–20.

The trees represent the brain's neurons. Dr. Paul MacLean—a neuroscientist whose work I will be referring to often—describes neurons as being structured like trees, with the axon acting as a trunk from which sprout at either end as many as a hundred branches and roots. At the tips of the neural branches and roots are tiny receiving and transmitting elements called dendrites.

The neural trees in the brain are positioned somewhat like links in a chain. At the point of the dendrites, when a "branch" of one neuron meets a "root" of another neuron, a synapse occurs, whereby an electrical signal jumps the gap between the two neurons, creating a (temporary) bridge. This temporary linkage gives the brain enormous flexibility because the patterns of neural linkages have the ability to shift instantly. Every now and then synaptic links hook up in novel ways, producing spontaneous new insights.

Neuroscientist Robert Thatcher, at the University of South Florida College of Medicine in Tampa, believes that our brain's neural networks of synaptic patterns undergo major restructurings (disruptions) every two years. In an article by Karen Wright in *Discover* magazine (October 1997) entitled "Babies, Bonds, and Brains," he suggests that these reorganizations happen not only because of our experiences but also in response to waves of nerve growth factor that sweep across the brain in two-year cycles, revamping up to one fifth of the brain's synaptic connections.

Neurons in the brain grow like trees in the ground because the brain's neurons emerge from its ground, Adamah. The matter of the brain is actually "seeded" with the potential to produce neurons, which is another aspect of human potential. "The number of connections between nerve cells in an infant's brain grows more than twenty-fold in the first few months of life," states Karen Wright in the same article:

> A two-year-old's brain contains twice as many of these connections, called synapses, as an adult's brain. Throughout early childhood these synapses multiply and are pruned away at a furious rate. Something directs this dynamic rewiring, and researchers have concluded that something is experience.

In other words, the *interplay* between a baby's awareness and its environment (inner and outer) is the experience, the something, that directs its explosive neural growth.

This is the nature of the tissue in the human brain, symbolized by the qualities of Gan-Eden, the Garden of Eden. A newborn's brain has the neurons it needs to regulate its body, but the neurons of experience are not yet present. An adult's brain, however, is so crowded with the neurons of experience that it resembles a jungle. The matter of the brain is present at birth, but the neurons of experience are not. What transpires during our development is the growth of neurons and neural networks, shaped through the interplay of outer environment and inner awareness. For us, that outer environment is now ruled predominantly by human culture and its social interactions, rather than by nature.

Neurons represent the *germ* of the brain, which can continually grow in humans, though the matter remains static, like a husk. The potential fertility (of thought) inherent in the growth of our neural networks is the same as that in every seed: indeterminate. Our brain can grow an indeterminate number of neurons and linkages. Most of us have plenty of neural networks, resulting in high intelligence. What we commonly lack is their integration, which produces an awareness of wholeness, a situation this story addresses and in which Adam's role is pivotal.

All information in the brain is shuttled throughout its interior on these linked neural networks that are self-generated (by Adamah) and self-organized (by Adam), forming a vast and intricate communication system consisting of neural trees and their dendrites. But, as Henry Poincaré stated, logic (Adam) is barren unless fertilized by intuition. Unfortunately, this Adam is orgainizing our neutral networks in ways that promote rigidity and alienation. He must be reoriented to include his opposite, Eve, in neutral functioning.

The Genesis story, though written as mythology, contains remarkable scientific and psychological correlations. For instance, the word *dendrite* is derived from a Greek word that means "tree." Modern scientific jargon uses the tree metaphor whenever the brain is described as a neural "forest" or "jungle." The garden analogy comes into play when we realize that a garden is where plants and trees are cultivated for food the way thoughts are cultivated in the mind—trees that are "good for food" become "food for thought"; all thinking travels a route through neural networks represented by the trees in Genesis.

The allegory of Adam in the Gan-Eden is rich and complex. This garden is not peaceful and bucolic but unstable and eruptive and therefore fertile and creative. Adam is thrown into this fertile instability, which will prevent him from fossilizing neurologically and perceptually. Within this unstable neural garden are the two famous trees, the tree of life and the tree of good (TVB) and evil (RA). The acronym TVB depicts the action of continuity in the brain, all the things we already know, provided by the brain's established neural structures. RA depicts the action of disruptive insight, the piercing of our armor of known phenomena with new, often revolutionary, yet previously unknown data that are our cosmic insurance policy against intellectual stagnation. The tree of the knowledge of TVB and RA (good and evil) depicts the universal struggle between the purveyors of new phenomena (RA/evil) and the guardians of the old order (TVB/good). It has been those guardians of the old patriarchal order who have interpreted this text. They are the ones, even today, who perceive RA as evil and who perceive women as the temptresses of evil. Yet RA is an element meant to safeguard us from adhering too fiercely to sacred-cow ideas that have lost their usefulness, in which we often become enmeshed, to our own detriment. Disruptions, RA, unsettle any static state of continuity we might wish to cling to and are a necessary element of psychological growth.

Although we do not yet perceive clearly the nature of the opposition of TVB/good and RA/evil because of our cultural biases toward disruption, we are immersed in life's pattern of the interplay between opposites. At this moment in time the interplay is especially noticeable as the disparate political and economic power between males and females. This interplay continually offers us the opportunity to grow, change, and become, but only if we digest the fruit. Obviously these insights offer a view of the elements in this myth—especially concerning the nature of RA (evil)—that is radically different. But it is radical only compared to the cultural biases with which we traditionally view these elements. In light of the brain's own activities, this new interpretation of Genesis makes remarkable sense.

ॐ *3* ॐ

A River Parted unto Four Heads: Brain Structure

In order to further explore the mythology of Genesis, the design of the brain itself must first be clarified. That design is stated metaphorically immediately after the verse in Genesis in which the two trees are introduced.

> *And a river went out of Eden to water the*
> *garden; and from thence it was parted, and*
> *became unto four heads.*
>
> GENESIS 2:10

Remember, Genesis 2 is a narrative of inner, not outer reality. A single river that becomes "four heads" is a mythological depiction of scientific fact: a single brain "parted" into four neural structures, or cortexes. Dr. Paul MacLean, former head of the department of brain evolution at the National Institutes of Mental Health, is a major figure in clarifying the brain's four structures, though I'm sure he has no idea they may apply to Genesis.

I encountered MacLean's material several years after beginning my studies with Qabalah. By then I had the basic idea figured out—that Genesis was narrating a hero's journey of integration—but I couldn't see the details. It wasn't until I'd incorporated MacLean's data about the brain's four neural structures that Genesis resonated at its deepest level.

Summing up his research in a "triune brain theory," MacLean concludes that the four neural structures of the human brain fit neatly into three categories. (I now disagree with that assessment, believing instead that the four correspond to *four* categories, a quadriune brain, but more on that later.) MacLean likens his triune theory to the old Roman teaching of rhetoric. It defined a primal mind, an emotional mind, and a rational mind. Furthermore, he states that the brain's three divisions form a hierarchy that mirrors the pattern of terrestrial evolution in human nervous system development. Result: The human brain contains a reptilian neural substrate, the *r-complex;* a mammalian neural substrate, the *limbic system,* or old mammalian brain; and a human neural substrate combining two units together, the *neocortex* and the *prefrontal cortex.*

MacLean asserts that each of these three brain components (made up of a total of four neural structures) has radically different physiological characteristics and chemistries resulting in wildly conflicting psychological agendas. He likens their behavior to three drivers behind the wheel—one reptilian, one mammalian, and one human—all wanting control of the vehicle (the body) for their specific agendas.

The four neural structures, or cortexes, housed together in the brain can cause us enormous confusion. Though we might assume that they work together, the truth is that they are more likely to be in conflict with one another. This conflict, I believe, lies at the root of most of our problems. Rather than being integrated, the brain is more like a wild beast dressed in a business suit on its way to Sunday Mass, sidetracked by a kitten it wants to pet. Driven by ancient power plays and lusts, modern yearnings for love and justice, as well as deep needs for affection and intimacy, the brain struggles with its own conflicting agendas, often disastrously. The result is all too apparent in the headlines, and often closer to home in our own confusing lives, where divorce, addiction, and depression may wreak havoc.

Until we can collectively become aware of the conflicting agendas of the four cortexes housed within our own skull, we will be unable to deal appropriately with the problems that erupt in our personal and social dwellings. Awareness of these neural structures is fundamental to understanding human nature and human behavior.

The brain embodies the pattern of wholeness, an integration of two opposites. In terms of not only cosmological, but also neural and psychological development, the two opposites are *continuity* and *disruption,* or *certainties* and *possibilities.* Certainties and continuities help us survive. But the disruptions of new possibilities help us grow and change, igniting the brain with new fertility and fecundity.

The Qabalists had great concern for brains that could become too rigid, subjected to the influence of too much continuity and not enough disruption. Such a brain is inflexible; instead of allowing growth and change, it uses its vast powers to maintain the status quo, guarding its hoard of information like a medieval dragon.

Dr. MacLean understands all too well how the opposing forces of certainties and possibilities interact in human brain development. His data, as well as the teaching of the Qabalists, will help us learn to integrate this four-part, dual-powered organism into a whole system with a unified purpose. That purpose is to actualize the brain's enormous potential, eventually leading to the discovery of wholeness, happiness, wisdom, and love.

Neural integration is not generally considered the soul's work. But Genesis is here to change our ideas about that. The soul's journey to completion takes place within the neural networks of the brain, not in some ethereal realm beyond description. In order to perceive wholeness, the brain and psyche must work together to integrate their diverse and opposing parts. We are the only heroes available for that task. It is a challenge of the greatest magnitude because there is no model to show us how. We often end up, as the title of a Sarah McLachlan album poetically has it, "fumbling toward ecstasy."

How, or even if, we integrate the parts of the brain depends entirely upon how we *perceive* those parts. As Arthur Young, inventor of the Bell helicopter and author of *The Geometry of Meaning*, expressed it, "The ultimate goal is to regain the whole by knowing how the parts fit together."* How we see the relationship among our neural parts determines whether or not we are capable of seeing the whole brain accurately.

Part of the process of reeducating the intellect involves scrutinizing the brain's individual neural structures. The following information offers a general overview.

PRIMAL MIND: THE REPTILIAN CORTEX

MacLean's work offers a bounty of information pertaining to the behaviors and chemistries of the reptilian substrate or r-complex, a clump of ganglia at the base of the brain dominated by two imperatives: procreation and territory. In his study of lizards, MacLean discovered twenty-four basic reptile behavior patterns that show up abundantly in modern humans, though we may be loath to admit it. In the following list formulated by MacLean (with my examples in parentheses), some behaviors are easily identifiable, while others need a little prompting before we recognize them in ourselves, such as *place preference behavior*, which is demonstrated by Archie Bunker in relation to his chair. The point of listing these behaviors is so we can learn to see them in ourselves and understand the significance of the r-complex's influence and purpose in our lives.

Reptilian Behaviors

1. Selecting and preparing a homesite (looking for a place to live, to go to school, and to work)

2. Establishing territory (buying or renting a home, moving into the dorm room)

3. Making trails (following favorite routes to favorite places such as stores or "watering holes")

*Arthur Bell, *The Geometry of Meaning* (New York: Delacorte Press, 1976), xv.

4. Marking territory (building a fence or putting posters and pictures on the walls)

5. Showing place preferences (sitting in routine seats at the breakfast or dinner table, parking in favorite parking places)

6. Patrolling territory (installing security lights, auto alarms, and house alarm systems; hiring security guards or calling the police)

7. Ritualistically displaying in defense of territory (using colors and adornments, such as flags, door numbers, and door signs)

8. Fighting formalized, intraspecies battles in defense of territory (playing football, fighting in gangs, fighting wars)

9. Triumphantly displaying a successful defense (dancing after a touchdown, teammates on a winning baseball team pouring champagne on each other)

10. Assuming distinctive postures and coloration in signaling surrender (displaying a white flag, sending an apology note along with flowers)

11. Foraging (shopping, berry picking, going to the farmer's market)

12. Hunting (stalking, doing research, crime detecting)

13. Homing (heading home after the hunt—or after a long day at work)

14. Hoarding (collecting art, coins, Beanie Babies, food, rubber bands, money, cars . . .)

15. Using defecation posts (creating foul-mouthed graffiti on walls, in books, on desks)

16. Forming social groups (organizing and joining teams, luncheons, staff meetings, church committees)

17. Establishing a social hierarchy through ritualistic display and other means (holding elections, inaugurations, coronations, awards ceremonies)

18. Greeting (saluting, waving, nodding head)

19. Grooming (needs no explanation)

20. Engaging in courtship, with displays using coloration and adornments (giving or wearing corsages, dressing fashionably or attractively)

21. Mating (needs no explanation)

22. Breeding and, in isolated cases, attending offspring (needs no explanation)

23. Flocking (attending a rock concert, shopping at a store's liquidation sale)

24. Migrating and subsequent colonizing (moving to a new city and establishing a neighborhood, moving to a new neighborhood and "gentrifying" it)

At the heart of Nietzsche's philosophy, states MacLean in *The Triune Concept of the Brain and Behavior,* was the "will to power," which neatly sums up the agenda of the r-complex:

> To see male rainbow lizards striving for dominance is like returning to the days of King Arthur. These animals have beautiful colors and like many lizards use head-bobbing and pushups in their territorial and courtship displays. In a contest, once the gauntlet is thrown down, the aggressive displays give way to violent combat, and the struggle is unrelenting. Twice we have seen dominant males humiliated in defeat. They lost their majestic colors, lapsed into a kind of depression, and died two weeks later.*

In humans the will to power is first seen in the "terrible twos" but is more apparent culturally as the engine that drives politics and corporate climbing. Recall the image of Mr. Gecko, the cold-blooded tycoon who was the lead character played by Michael Douglas in the movie *Wall Street.* The r-complex also plays a role in disorders such as anorexia, where willpower is used to overcome the basic desire to eat.

---

*Paul MacLean, "The Triune Concept of the Brain and Behavior." In the *Hincks Memorial Lectures* (Toronto: University of Toronto Press, 1973), 317.

Results of experiments on monkeys convinced MacLean that the r-complex also plays a special role in other kinds of mammalian behavior, including that of humans. His findings indicate that in animals as widely separated as reptiles and primates, the r-complex is implicated in the "organized expression of ritualistic, non-verbal (prosematic) behavior"—body language with specific symbolic intent, such as flipping off someone. Lizards use head-bobbing and push-ups in territorial challenge displays as well as courtship. How often do we witness human males strutting on the beach, flexing their muscles, hoping to attract the attention of nearby females? Or what about the military salute as a stylized version of head-bobbing?

Such gestures, though partially organized by the r-complex, are also culturally specific, referring to the fuzzy boundaries of social territory. Nodding the head to indicate yes in our culture may mean no in another. Understanding culturally specific behaviors, such as those abundantly observed in any Catholic church (kissing the Crucifix, kneeling) or through Western social orders (the crowning of monarchs, swearing in of judges, sentencing of criminals, saluting the flag), helps us identify with our social group. Other gestures abounding in human life are not ones that we generally think of in reptilian terms. A favorite of defiant children is sticking out the tongue, which is reminiscent of reptilian tongue flicking. Displaying personal triumph by pulling down the fist, as Macauley Culkin does in the hit movie *Home Alone,* is seldom misunderstood, at least not in our culture.

Gestures such as these—dealing with power, territory, and courtship—convey information without the use of words or language. Similar gestures, though perhaps with different implications, can be found in all cultures. It doesn't take much reflection to realize we humans use such gestures extensively, helping us to recognize that the r-complex is intrinsic to human behavior, even though such behaviors may be organized by cultural preference.

Beyond gesture, appearance can also hearken to reptilian roots. In Hollywood portrayals, the devil looks surprisingly reptilian, as do many villains. We even resort to using reptilian metaphors to highlight offensive traits in descriptions such as "cold-blooded killers" and "ice queens."

An old television special, *The Visitors,* was particularly vivid. It depicted peaceful, human-looking aliens from a dry planet who came to earth in huge flying saucers and seemed only to want a little water. In actuality, the aliens were reptiles in disguise. Concealing their true identities with elaborate latex human masks, they enjoyed feasting on the delicacies of hamsters and humans. Reptiles in human disguise is a powerful mythological image. Is this one of the psyche's creative methods of self-illumination regarding our own neural structure?

Observations of reptiles reveal that they are slaves to routine, precedent, and ritual. MacLean learned that the r-complex shows up in a few basic human proclivities, namely slavish conformance to routine and old, familiar ways of doing things (evidenced in bureaucracy), observation of personal day-to-day rituals and superstitions (even to the extent of obsessions or compulsions), obeisance to precedent (seen in judicial proceedings), ceremonially reenacting responses to partial representations of either alive or inanimate images (saluting the flag or the president), and carrying out all manner of deceptions (lying, cheating, submitting false information on forms, and, especially, denying).

Such behaviors are based on *continuity,* a lack of change that proves to have survival value. If a roundabout route to a food supply has proved safe, why risk a shorter route? If believing in Jesus or Buddha means you won't go to hell or incur bad karma, why risk not believing? In legal matters, attorneys spend endless time and energy searching for precedents in order to support their case. The r-complex is driven by the forces of continuity to seek safety and self-preservation. That means: Don't take risks and don't disrupt the routine. Sound familiar?

MacLean concludes that the r-complex is good at protecting us from known dangers but is incapable of integrating new information, however advantageous it may prove to be. The r-complex, he warns, is not a good learner. Actually, beyond certain innate survival and predatory instincts, it doesn't learn at all, which is why it prefers keeping things the way they are. Much of our fear of new situations is derived from neurochemistries controlled by the r-complex. This provides a major source of psychological conflict for us because, as we will see, other parts of the brain are designed to learn and have a built-in desire to do so.

Risk-taking is essential to balanced psychological development. We cannot live a fully human life without taking risks and testing the unknown because that is how we discover and develop unrealized potential. Those who refuse to take risks, who merely exist in an endless routine of survival, depicted in the 1960s as the dreaded image of *the establishment,* paint themselves into a reptilian corner of rigid continuity, sacrificing unrealized potential for safety.

Whenever we feel unreasonably self-protective, it is most likely that our r-complex is reacting to something new or unknown that it perceives as a dangerous threat to survival. It responds by releasing powerful hormones that trigger the "fight or flight" reflex. However, the other, newer neural structures in the brain are better equipped to assess situations and are able to produce neurochemicals that can calm the r-complex. In many cases we actually have to tell the r-complex things are okay before it will settle down. In such cases we use phrases like, "Don't get your feathers ruffled," a metaphor that recalls the theory that birds evolved from reptiles whose scales evolved into feathers.

Although MacLean's research proves that we all have an r-complex, how each of us deals with its neural patterns, chemistry, and agenda can vary widely. Do we integrate them into whole brain functioning or alienate and deny them?

Hitler's Third Reich showed a prevalence for reptilian traits: the ritualized, goose-stepping march of the SS, systematic predation of the Jews, slavish conformance to ritualistic displays involving the swastika, and on and on, right down the list MacLean compiled. Modern gang behavior is also rife with reptilian patterns, especially its hierarchical power structure and predatory practices.

An r-complex that is either alienated or worshiped can be incredibly destructive, both socially and psychologically. Similarly, a brain that has not successfully integrated the higher neural structures is one that relies disproportionately on the behavior and chemistry of the r-complex for survival. Serial killers, stalkers, and terrorists exhibit the extreme examples of predatory behaviors that originate in the r-complex.

On the other hand, a detective relentlessly pursuing a killer and a researcher pursuing an elusive bacterial killer are both using the same predatory instincts as the criminal or terrorist. The predation impulse is not in itself a "bad" or "evil" trait. How we use it determines its effect on ourselves and others. It behooves us to educate ourselves as to the source of such behaviors and learn why most of us do not resort to social predation in its various forms but instead learn to integrate predatory instincts in healthy ways. Just as important is to learn what is at the root of those few who fail to integrate these in positive ways. Most important of all is spotting these individuals early and initiating integrative therapy, which could prove to prevent later criminal or destructive behavior, with its high financial and emotional costs.

Since time immemorial human beings have been searching for the roots of what we perceive as evil. Along with MacLean, I think we will find them in the r-complex, with its predatory and deceptive patterns functioning through specific neurochemistries. Those of us who integrate such patterns and neurochemistries in wholesome ways learn to use them, for example, to "hunt" for a better, more fulfilling life. Psychological integration at the earliest possible age is the key.

EMOTIONAL MIND: THE LIMBIC SYSTEM

The limbic system is a small neural area surrounding and perched atop the r-complex, from which it evolved and differentiated. It is the first of the brain's neural structures to receive *every piece* of incoming data from all the senses and other brain areas. It then transfers this staggering amount of data to other parts of the brain for further processing.

Researchers are developing a new respect for the limbic system because they have discovered it to be the first neural substrate in the brain designed to learn. Clinical and experimental findings of the past sixty years indicate that the limbic system experiences its information through emotional feelings that guide behavior required for self-preservation and preservation of the species. Its learning apparatus initially develops through the relationship between a parent—usually the mother—and her offspring. This deep relationship development is often referred to as *bonding* because the neurochemistry of trust is so strong that it *binds* us to those with whom we associate it.

When mothers kiss their babies, cuddle them, murmur to them, caress them, and otherwise attend to them, the neurochemistry of love is produced both in the mother and in the infant through limbic system functions. Attentiveness is one basis for trust and is intricately intertwined in the neurochemistry of bonding. This attentiveness, or lack of it, has a powerful effect on the way the brain organizes and transfers all social and psychological information.

Limbic system functions have deep ties to auditory channels. Early mammals were small and made their living by night while dinosaurs ruled the world by day. Being nocturnal, their sense of hearing became invaluable to their survival and to the survival of their young.

Women are generally better than men when it comes to processing linguistic information because the nurturing emotions involved in child rearing enhance the evolution of women's connections to auditory channels in the limbic system. There are exceptions, of course, and men can learn to become every bit as emotionally and linguistically responsive as women if that is their intention.

Because the limbic system is the transfer station for all incoming data, and because it processes information in terms of emotional feelings, its data-transferring processes are organized, presumably, according to our own feelings about that particular data. Patriarchal attitudes toward feelings of vulnerability and emotional needs tend to be less than validating. Consequently, many of us suppress our vulnerabilities and feelings in order to be accepted, depressing limbic system functions in psychological development.

Monotheistic religious leaders insist that God loves us and we should love God. But it isn't God's love we need because it isn't God who has the potential to abandon, alienate, neglect, or shame us, as our parents, friends, enemies, and lovers can, and often do. Only other people can treat us that way and it is such treatment that has disastrous effects emotionally, psychologically, and socially. It seems that it is love from other humans we need, not love from God. The reason we are admonished to love our neighbor is because the characteristics of whole systems, especially whole social systems, dictate it. We need to be loved by others so we won't feel abandoned, alienated, or neglected. But we ourselves need to love others because that diminishes the potential for violence in us. Love and the potential for violence (directed by feelings of fear and hatred) are both processed initially in the limbic system—and there is no God there, only feelings.

Psychology and psychiatry are both professions based on the need to be aware of our feelings and how they are processed in the brain. Therapists are concerned mainly with how a patient feels about any given subject. This information about the limbic system's functions makes the reason for this focus on feelings obvious: They have a huge impact on both our behavior *and* our neural organization. Talking to a therapist can help rewire the brain's neural networks for healthier behavior if it can get us in touch with feelings that had previously been alienated through neglect, abandonment, or otherwise, but which nevertheless may still have a powerful effect on how the brain is sending information to other parts of itself.

The limbic system generates the strong feelings of conviction we often attach to our beliefs. Many people mistake these feelings of conviction for absolute truths. Following their convictions, people have been known to engage in mass suicide, ritualistic killings, or even terrorist acts, such as those of antiabortionists, who kill doctors who perform abortions, or those of the terrorists who committed the disastrous acts of September 11, 2001.

We have the power to change our convictions, but it requires deep levels of self-awareness. A recent article in my local paper told the story of an ex–Ku Klux Klan member who spent several years in prison. While incarcerated he had time to think and reevaluate his feelings. He began to talk about how he was raised, especially the effect his father's attitudes had on the development of his own moral code. After much soul searching, he finally realized that his own feelings were quite different from his father's. That recognition deeply affected his behavior. When released from prison, he denounced the Klan and has since been encouraging others to abandon their racial hatred. The enormous changes he went through began with examining his feelings originating in the limbic system and powerfully affecting his behavior, attitudes, and convictions.

The most potent of the limbic system's functions, however, are perhaps the most overlooked and least understood: the functions concerned with personal identity and memory. The limbic system processes data coming from two sources: the internal private world of the self (feelings, convictions, and attitudes) and the external, shared world of culture and relationships. This has enormous ramifications both socially and psychologically.

Memory—and our feelings of personal identity—depends on the brain's ability to combine and integrate internal feelings and attitudes with external stimuli. What makes us unique as individuals is this combination of private/public neural interaction. When we consider that only the information from the external world is publicly available to everyone, whereas the information from the private, internal world is available only to the self, we begin to have a deeper respect for the processing skills of the primitive limbic system. It has enormous power to affect our psychological and spiritual growth.

I am always struck, when contemplating the powerful functions of the limbic system with regard to personal growth and identity, by the image of Jesus being born in a stable, because a stable is where (nonhuman) mammals are typically housed. The limbic system is a mammalian structure. Could the imagery of Jesus' birth be conveying mythological information about the brain, identity, and memory?

Jesus declared that we need to be "born again." Could not this new birth be an act of remembering our mammalian heritage, the behavior patterns involved in affection, attentiveness, nurturing, and protection orchestrated through limbic neural structures and chemistries? Such behaviors and chemistries form the foundation of trust, and trust is what heals the emotional pains of abandonment, rejection, and shame that too often become entangled in patriarchal paradigms.

The manufacture of experiences pertaining to personal identity and memory is made possible by the limbic system's function of combining both internal and external data. This is critical in our personal development and plays an enormous role in the hero's journey to integration, autonomy, and fertility of mind.

Self-evaluations—such as how we feel about ourselves, whether or not we like or respect ourselves, inflate or deflate our value, and make ourselves feel better when others make us feel bad—are reflections that begin in the limbic system. Usually generated initially in early childhood through interactions with primary caretakers, these self-evaluations often deeply affect how we relate to ourselves and others for the rest of our lives. For example, if we feel inadequate (because we were neglected in childhood), our ability to grow psychologically is sabotaged. This is why so many people talk about their parents in therapy; they are trying to overcome the feelings of inadequacy acquired in childhood that still affect them as adults. On the other hand, feeling overly confident sabotages our growth in another way: We fail to perceive our *actual* inadequacies so that we can work on them. Such examples indicate that integrating and balancing feelings promotes healthy psychological growth, perhaps because it exercises the limbic system's interactive qualities.

Before we move on to the next two neural structures of the brain, one other piece of data must be mentioned concerning the r-complex and limbic system: Neither has a neural foundation for producing language. It has been thought that they combine to function in what has often been referred to as the *subconscious*. But that analysis hinders integration. The limbic system and r-complex are not subconscious;

merely nonlinguistic. Because they cannot communicate their contents through words, they often resort to other means of communication to make themselves known and felt, such as dream imagery, behavior patterns, willpower, and emotions. Unable to articulate their own presence, much less any disorder that may afflict them, they often trigger seemingly bizarre behavior patterns to make their presence known and felt (such as kids carving themselves up with razor blades).

Primitive though they may be, these two oldest neural structures of the brain contain valuable information not only for our survival but also for our psychological well-being. Part of any integration process thus needs to involve the articulation of dysfunctional patterns that may arise from the compartmentalization and alienation of the contents of the r–complex and limbic system. In twelve-step programs everywhere, such patterns are now being recognized and articulated through terms such as *codependency* and *abandonment issues* and can be reintegrated through healing processes. This is an ongoing creative effort by healers and helps us all better understand the brain and our own processes of psychological growth and integration.

RATIONAL MIND: THE NEOCORTEX

Most of us are familiar with the image of the brain as a convoluted walnut-shaped mass of gray matter. This mass is the cortex, specifically the neocortex. *Neo* means "new" in Latin; the neocortex is a *new* mammalian cortex, compared to the *old* mammalian limbic system from which it evolved. In true evolutionary fashion, the neocortex expanded out of the third subdivision of the limbic system (from an area involving vision) and is organized almost exclusively around *external visual stimuli*. It became progressively larger in primates—presumably promoted by the hand-eye coordination needed to swing successfully through trees—expanding to its greatest size in human beings. Hand-eye coordination culminates in the various skills involved in technological innovation, especially those leading to tool making and literacy. Devoted to the production of symbolic language and artifacts, the neocortex is associated with the functions of technology and its subsequent processing of symbols involved in reading, writing, and arithmetic. It houses most of the attributes we usually ascribe to the human intellect.

A major distinction between this "neo" cortex and the older two neural structures is that it has the potential for language and they do not. Therefore, the major distinction between other animals and human beings, or so the prevailing scientific thinking goes, is that we have language and they don't. The potential for language, along with bipedalism, which developed concurrently with the neocortex, is what separates and distinguishes humans from the rest of the evolutionary masses, or so we assume. For the last hundred years, science has firmly tied human identity to neocortical functioning.

It is up to the neocortex, with its linguistic arsenal, to provide words for the two older, nonlinguistic neural structures. But—in contrast to the limbic system's ability to process data originating from within ourselves—the cells of the neocortex process only data streaming in from the outer world. As we will see, this distinction between the limbic system and the neocortex is crucial, not only to our understanding of the brain, but but also to understanding the hero's journey described in Genesis. Because the focus of the neocortex is on the processing of external visual stimuli, it is unable to look inward and see those other parts of the brain at work. This presents a multitude of problems regarding self-awareness and personal growth, which may be another reason Adam—the mythological representation of the neocortex—needs a helpmate.

The particular way in which the neocortex processes external visual stimuli into meaning (and metaphor) through language is clarified in a master's thesis written by Rob Hanford (University of California at Berkeley, 1979). Hanford discovered that our bipedal posture coupled with our stereoscopic vision—the two major sensory orientations of the neocortex—have an enormous impact on our symbolic thinking processes. Hanford's paper reveals previously hidden information-processing patterns in the brain, first remarked upon by Benjamin Whorf, an insurance adjuster turned linguist.

Western European languages, including English, have the peculiar habit of using an imaginary space as a setting to talk about the inner landscape of thought and imagination, though inner awareness has no spatial orientation whatsoever. As speakers of these languages, Whorf noted, we tend to describe aspects of being according to the positions of objects in space. We describe ideas and opinions as if they are objects located on a plane. Thus ideas are said to be "far apart" or "close together," "parallel to one another" or "way out of line," "leaning the same way," or "headed in opposite directions." We are constantly judging ideas by "plain" sense because it is *plane* sense that we are actually using.

That we speak of one domain of experience in terms of another is neither surprising nor unusual, states Hanford. It is the basic foundation of metaphor and is intrinsic to the human nervous system. What's remarkable about it is that most of us never take it into consideration; we don't take note of the metaphorical origins of our symbolic thinking processes *in* our unique posture, which developed concurrently with the neocortex as we climbed down from the trees in the shrinking forests and took up residence on the vast *plains* of Africa. When we moved onto those plains we stood up, giving ourselves a view of the world that we now interpret through *plane* geometry and metaphors such as those just mentioned.

Space is a critical factor in processing information from the unique perspective of human bipedalism combined with stereoscopic vision, the two key ingredients in the neocortex's perceptual interpretation of events. In fact, the shape of the imaginary space paradigm we use to perceive reality, Hanford suggests, is itself noted in the etymology of the word *reality,* derived from a Latin word meaning "pertaining to the thing or matter." Generally, in our Western worldview, a "thing" is real only so long as it can be proved to matter. Hanford notes that we bring such intangibles as ideas and opinions into existence by presenting them to others as if they are objects that "stand forth" or "appear" in space.

In order to initiate a conversation, we first "raise" or "bring up" a matter to discuss and then "state" the point we want to make. A *statement* means "a place to stand." How many of us resort to the ubiquitous "I can't stand that" when referring to something we dislike, or, as parents, use "I won't stand for that" when referring to our children's outrageous behavior? We are often called upon to "stand up" for our rights or beliefs. And what about "understanding"? Such references are seldom recognized as linguistic metaphors linked to our unique posture, which we inherited from the hominids during a period of several million years when the neocortex was undergoing a huge expansion.

In order to learn how to stand, our body had to learn first to raise up and then stabilize its four major weight segments: head, thorax, hips, and legs. The alignment of the centers of gravity of each of these four segments yields the most stable stacking. That's why standing up straight, or upright, is said to be correct posture, the *right* way to stand. So, too, there are an infinite number of angles in a circle, yet only one is defined as a *right* angle. Is it coincidence that 90 degrees is the angle at which we stand in relation to the ground? We also express this sense of balance, acquired exclusively through bipedal posture, in metaphors that correlate *correct* with *right*.

In order to *build a case,* one must *stack up* a *body of evidence* in alignment with a gravitational field in which the speaker, and those in agreement, are assumed to *stand*. When an argument *falls flat on its face,* those who agreed with it are thought to do the same. Participants in a conversation will agree on a matter so long as they feel able to *stand* by it, but the moment a stated frame of reference leans too far from their own sense of what's right, they tend to feel *upset* by the idea and in danger of being *put down* or *losing face.* The word *tolerate* comes from the Latin *tollere,* which means "to lift up" or "to raise." Ideas of which we are intolerant are those we cannot *stand.* When two people grow intolerant of each other, they are said to have a *falling out.*

As these examples illustrate, *plane sense* is an important element of our culture's system of verbal interaction. It is by these *grounds* that we establish communication. So too the words *reason* and *rational* are equated with understandings that are thought to be *even* or *level* with one another. People who have similar reasons are thought to be *in correspondence* with each other. By the same measure, those understandings that are *at odds* with a viewpoint are perceived as *irrational,* which in Latin means "not in ratio." Anyone who stands by that inclination is obviously quite *incorrect*. We agree that a statement is true only when the rationale behind it is *equivalent* (from the Latin for "equal in value") to our own.

Our bipedal posture is intertwined with the laws of gravity. Hence, Newtonian thinking, based on *rationale* and reason, is rooted in the certainty that gravity provides. With quantum investigation and chaos theory, another dimension to reality is introduced—energy, which does not behave according to the laws of gravity. Mass behaves according to the laws of gravity and certainty; energy does not. The neocortex often has great difficulty understanding the behavior of energy because it has no point of reference yet. Its interpretations of data and events are based, almost entirely, on Newtonian certainties—that is, the certainties of mass behaving according to the laws of gravity by which we stand upright.

The way the neocortex interprets data—through the certainties of "rationale and reason"—has been the basis of the conviction that science expresses the highest form of intelligence and that progress in the social and political spheres will be made as we apply scientific laws to society. Yet we have just seen how the basis of such "certainty" is formulated on the behavior *only* of mass and gravity. It does not include the behavior of energy, which is only just recently coming under the scrutiny of science. Until science can adequately describe the behavior of energy, I'm afraid it won't be very successful in applying the laws of science to our behavior, which includes enormous amounts of energy. Amazingly, Genesis provides this missing information. Actually, this information has always been provided through what we loosely term *spirituality,* which *is* energy—at least one of the potentials of energy. And with that, we can finally introduce the newest neural structure of the brain.

A NEURAL ADDITION?

MacLean states that the neocortex sports a nifty neural "add-on," like a family room or bedroom we might build onto our house. This neural addition is the *prefrontal cortex,* that portion of the brain sitting directly behind the forehead. The prefrontal cortex (often referred to as the frontal lobes) together with the neocortex make up the third division, the human portion, of MacLean's triune formula.

MacLean's speculation about the frontal lobes as an "addition" to the neocortex, tying them up together in the same categorical knot, is a speculation with which most evolutionary scientists agree. Qabalah, however, does not—a point that is made emphatically in Genesis, if you understand its coded information and the meaning of its mythological imagery. We'll come back to this critical difference momentarily.

The frontal lobes are highly intelligent, but in a radically different way from the neocortex, representing a revolutionary new potential within the neurology of human beings. Most of us, however, have little inkling of the true value of this newest component of the brain. As MacLean points out and other research substantiates, our intelligence quotient, or IQ, as it is measured on standard tests, is totally *unaffected* by loss of the frontal lobes. (This is how medical science used to rationalize the use of lobotomies, now abolished but not before Egas Moniz received a 1949 Nobel for perfecting, and promoting them.) MacLean maintains that the type of intelligence the frontal lobes display, though not traditionally measured, is every bit as important as the rational intelligence of the neocortex—or perhaps more important. Without the frontal lobes, MacLean claims, we lose much of what we generally consider to be human about ourselves. MacLean asserts that the frontal lobes add a much needed heart to the cool deductive machinery of the neocortex, which would be a bit of a calculating monster had it been left alone to dominate the neural scene.

According to MacLean, the special talent of the frontal lobes lies in one specific neural trait that gives rise to a plethora of human qualities and potentials. His research indicates that the prefrontal cortex is the only neural structure in the brain to *look inward,* which is perhaps why images of the third eye are often painted on the forehead. Like the neocortex, the prefrontal cortex has a visual apparatus, but its focus is opposite that of the outward-gazing neocortex. This inward focus gives the frontal lobes a revolutionary and unique perspective that science has barely detected, though it has been part of our neural anatomy for perhaps as long as two hundred thousand years.

In close proximity to the frontal lobes are parts of the limbic system, the only other cortex in the brain with an apparatus for discerning internal data. The major distinction between the internal devices of the limbic system and those of the frontal lobes is that the latter use extensions of *visual* mechanisms whereas the limbic system relies on feelings and emotions. Evidence indicates that through the close association of these two cortexes, we obtain the "gut feelings" required for identifying with others, which amounts to a neurological basis for empathy.

Patients with frontal lobe damage are notorious for their inability to anticipate the consequences of their actions within a social context. They lack insight into the motivations of others, and even of themselves, so they cannot plan their behavior successfully within group dynamics. Neanderthals, though they had brains as big as ours, had less frontal lobe area. Scientists have concluded that they relied on opportunity rather than planning for their survival; no one, for example, has yet discovered a Neanderthal ice pit for storing meat, whereas such pits are abundant at prehistoric human sites.

This ability to plan for the future is *foresight,* something the neocortex, with its rational and logical capacities, cannot and does not provide, but with which the frontal lobes are naturally endowed. A famous case illustrating the role of the frontal lobes in providing foresight is that of twenty-five-year-old Phineas Gage, a railroad foreman in 1848. While preparing a blast, Gage was tamping a charge of powder that accidentally exploded and drove the tamping rod—a metal bar three feet long and one inch thick—up through his left cheek and out the top of his skull near the front of his head, all but destroying his frontal lobes. Miraculously, he was able to function afterward and explain what happened. A stormy recovery followed, however, in which he displayed a distressing change of character, so much so that his friends later said he was "no longer Gage." His body seemed intact but his character had definitely changed.

J. M. Harlow, Gage's doctor, described him in the 1848 publication of the *Boston Medical and Surgical Journal* as "fitful, irreverent, indulging at times in the grossest profanity . . . manifesting little deference for his fellows, impatient of restraint or advice . . . at times perniciously obstinate, yet capricious and vacillating. . . . Previous to his injuries, though untrained in the schools, he possessed a well-balanced mind."

Without foresight provided by the frontal lobes, Gage lost his ability to make good decisions for himself and to control behaviors that have social significance. He could no longer judge the consequences of his own actions with any future perspective.

We are often like Gage when it comes to understanding the implications of our behavior on the future of our natural, living environment. Corporations are notorious for lacking environmental foresight, often thinking they can continue to cut down trees forever or drill oil forever and that the consequences will not be devastating, or that we can poison the air, water, and topsoil with toxic pollutants, fertilizers, herbicides, and so forth without suffering any negative consequences in the future. In our social and political agendas we often seem unable to judge the consequences of our own behavior within any future context. As yet another high school student guns down several of his classmates, the NRA goes on advocating the freedom to carry, own, and use handguns, automatic weapons, and the like, with few restrictions. In such cases, like Gage we are functioning without foresight. Unlike Gage, we have not had a metal rod blown through our brain—at least, not a physical one.

Our problem is similar to that of Gage because we lack an understanding of and appreciation for the prefrontal cortex and the kind of information it could provide us if we were more in touch with its methods of communication. Because we aren't, however, the r-complex and neocortex are often running the show. The r-complex is an absolute fanatic about maintaining the status quo, so the NRA continues to intimidate and propagandize, corporations continue to pollute, and governments continue to gather data. Meanwhile the environment, both ecological and social, deteriorates all around us. Like Gage, what most of us do about it is rant and rave because either our frontal lobes aren't functioning or we aren't paying attention to their messages. The prefrontal cortex, because it has not yet been recognized or categorized properly, has also not been educated, trained, or developed to give us some essential information about ourselves, information we desperately need if we are going to heal the ills of ourselves and of our society.

Included within the dossier of our personal information is that intangible sense of self that we refer to as the soul, spirit, or psyche. Information about this part of ourselves reveals that its substance is not matter, but something else, something we have a great difficulty defining or identifying through the use of symbols. The Bible refers to it as *light*. The frontal lobes, I believe, contain the potential that we usually refer to as soul, spirit, or psyche, especially in terms such as "the irrepressible human spirit." This is the intelligence and potential we use when we search deeply for meaning or when we overcome incredible social odds, such as surviving situations of enormous suffering inflicted by other humans in concentration camps or in prisoner-of-war camps, or surviving the devastation of terrorist bombings. This is a much different form of intelligence from that offered by the neocortex.

When searching deep within ourselves to understand our problems or to make sense of a world that seems dangerously out of balance, we are using the intelligence and potentials of the frontal lobes, the personal and social dimensions of human life. The frontal lobes utilize insight, intuition, and foresight—elements pertaining to light—to gather and process information about ourselves and our social world. They offer this type of intelligence, sometimes quite remarkably, often in spite of our own resistance to it.

Let's investigate this further.

Foresight is the foundation of altruism. The golden rule is "Do unto others as you would have others do unto you." The frontal lobes, MacLean declares, demonstrate definite altruistic tendencies. He goes so far as to say that with their addition, ". . . we seem to be acquiring the mental stuff of which we imagine angels are made."*

Is it merely coincidence that many religious and spiritual rituals, goals, and practices such as prayer, meditation, and yoga seem to be designed to realize and develop potentials and powers housed in the prefrontal cortex—powers that look inward to the self, the soul, spirit, or psyche—and that these powers together may form the basis of foresight and insight because their substance is light? Is this not information we should trust?

Noted neural researcher Antonio Damasio claims that the prefrontal cortex contains a neurology devoted to the personal and social dimensions of reasoning. This includes information about human essence, about behavioral and psychological patterns. Are these not the dimensions involved in personal growth?

Many religious leaders assume they know what God wants from us. What if we stop thinking about God and instead begin observing our own behavior toward others, our own thoughts within our own mind, and our own feelings within our own experience? This is what the Qabalah proposes: that we change our focus and pay attention to our instrument of perception and interpretation—namely, the human brain.

---

*Paul MacLean, "A Triune Concept of the Brain and Behavior." In the *Hincks Memorial Lectures* (Toronto: University of Toronto Press, 1973), 342.

If we look inward, as the frontal lobes allow us to, and stop making assumptions about what we find there, what *will* we find there? This, according to the Qabalists, is our work, our first vocation, mythologically portrayed in Gensis as the hero's journey.

Genesis proposes that the way in which we become familiar with ourselves, with the inner workings of our minds, psyches, and souls, and with how such workings affect our behavior, is by eating the fruit that opens our eyes—the inward-looking eyes of the frontal lobes. The distinction of the frontal lobes is that they do not process information through the five senses, but rather through an entirely different information-gathering system—inner light—that provides insight into the personal and social dimensions of reasoning.

Is it any coincidence that those among us who have been diagnosed with ADD or ADHD and who thus have compromised awareness and control over their behavior and social interactions also display the least neural activity in their frontal lobes, as evidenced by MRI scans?

Children diagnosed as hyperactive are prescribed the drug Ritalin, a brain stimulant. I have often wondered: Why give a brain stimulant to someone diagnosed as hyperactive? Brain research reveals why. Such children are functioning with low arousal in their frontal lobes. The portion of their brain that looks inward and gives them the emotional and social feedback they need in order to plan their own behavior appropriately, is, for all intents and purposes, asleep.

A study presented in a documentary titled *Minds to Crime* on the Learning Channel tied the frontal lobes to the behavior of children diagnosed with ADD and also implicated the frontal lobes in the criminal behavior of two thousand prison inmates whose brains were scanned using MRI techniques. The scans, based on blood flow, revealed that a whopping 98 percent of the inmates functioned with low arousal levels in the frontal lobes, indicated by decreased blood flow.

I do not present these data as a way of excusing the behavior of criminals, but only as a way of explaining it. I also believe that criminal tendencies are largely due, though not exclusively, to abusive parenting—

that is, parenting that relies on pain, shaming, or other psychologically damaging techniques to control children's behavior. For the developing psyche in children, family interactions are the most intimate and powerful aspects of the personal and social dimensions of life. When the administering of physical, emotional, intellectual, or spiritual pain is used instead of basic parenting techniques, the damage can last a lifetime and often exhibits itself in criminal and/or dysfunctional behavior. While the Learning Channel program mentioned above detailed the mishaps of a six-year-old boy with alarming antisocial traits who had never been abused by his parents, he is the exception, suffering since birth from mixed-up neural wiring. Most of us are born with brains highly organized for social interaction. As babies we like to please our parents. We usually resort to antisocial behavior only when our environment is abusive or neglectful, as a way of drawing attention to our problems.

Certainly people do not wish to become abusive parents, and certainly those parents who are abusive do not intend to produce criminality in their children. But research now shows that a simple lack of affection can have deep implications in childhood development, neurochemically as well as neurophysiologically. How much more of an impact would continual physical and emotional pain produce? Research on adults shows that criminal behavior is almost always linked to early child abuse, with pain being the element that makes any action or behavior abusive. When one person inflicts pain on another—whether physical, emotional, sexual, or psychological—it always impacts both the personal and the social dimensions of our lives.

The personal and social dimensions of intelligence are addressed by the frontal lobes and deeply affect our sense of self-worth and self-esteem. The fact that abuse and neglect may be enormous factors in criminal behavior should come as no surprise if we understand how the frontal lobes work. This is not to imply that all criminal behavior is due to parental abuse and/or neglect, nor that all who are abused will come to behave criminally. Obviously personal neurology and psychology are huge factors as well. But I think the majority of those incarcerated would agree with the sentiment I heard one inmate voice, as he indicated a model of normal, attentive, appropriate parenting: "What do you think we would have turned out to be like if we'd had parents like that?"

Without the frontal lobes functioning at optimum levels, we can't make good decisions for our lives or plan well for the future, nor can we empathize with others or exercise altruistic qualities. It's obvious that the personal and social dimensions of reasoning are invaluable to us, yet they are seldom given the attention they deserve. In fact, these activities and potentials aren't measured, tested, or even, in some cases, recognized.

This, then, is the paradox. Though the frontal lobes contain enormous potential wisdom for personal and social transformation, they lack any formal recognition, development, or training. In such a scenario, the neocortex's three-thousand-year head start via academic curriculum—which amounts to a muscle-building course for the activities of certainty, rationale, and reason—constantly overwhelms the delicate potentials of the frontal lobes, resulting in confusion, denial, apathy, depression, and a host of related spiritual and psychological problems. The neocortex, backed by academic development and its assumption of certainties and authorities, has assumed the role of master in our lives and has become, instead, a bad servant because it knows nothing of the personal and social dimensions of awareness, the light hidden within. To this day, the prefrontal cortex, our angelic potential, is still struggling for recognition.

Finally, this lack of recognition, training, and development of the prefrontal cortex, which is encapsulated in the relationship between Adam and Eve and more specifically in the image of Eve herself, is told in a story meant to transform us through that recognition.

THE RIVER THAT BECAME "FOUR HEADS"

MacLean's information is invaluable to our understanding of Genesis. We need to alter it a bit, however, and realize that the frontal lobes are *not* an addition to the neocortex, but rather a radical new portion of the brain with its own agenda, the only authentic human agenda on the planet. Viewing the prefrontal cortex from the perspective of an addition predisposes us to thinking that its neurology represents a continuation, more or less, of the neocortex. According to the Qabalists, that would be the worst mistake we could make.

If the four neural structures of the brain are to be grouped in any fashion, it would be one in which the oldest three cortexes are placed in one category together, with the frontal lobes alone residing in another. The oldest three cortexes—the r-complex, limbic system, and neocortex—represent the evolutionary continuum of a sensory-organized nervous system. They evolved through the primary input of sensory stimulation—taste, smell, hearing, touch, and vision—signals that arise in the *outer* world.

By contrast, instead of reacting to sensory stimuli, the frontal lobes are designed to process and make plans according to that information. They operate primarily from human input. Such input is the seventh day of symbol processing. In other words, the frontal lobes are designed to respond to personal and social information. They interpret light from the *inner* world of the self, psyche, soul, and spirit, which they process through insight, intuition, and foresight. This is the discontinuous leap in our brain's neural functions: from sensory to nonsensory, from outer to inner.

The transition from a reactive nervous system to a proactive nervous system is the theme of Genesis and the hero's journey. A proactive nervous system disrupts the patterns of the (evolutionary) reactive nervous system. Evolution's sensory nervous system is reactive because it is designed to react to outer stimuli, which the senses are designed to read. A proactive nervous system, on the other hand, uses foresight—inner awareness—to plan its own environment.

The frontal lobes don't given us a pronounced, easily recognizable new physical trait, like standing up or gaining language. Instead, they impart a subtle new shape to our skull and offer us a vast new *internal* neural potential that becomes activated during the personal and social examination of our nature. This potential is deeply influenced by how we think about and organize ourselves. (It may come as a shock to some, but patriarchal authoritarian social organization is not the only pattern available.) Frontal lobe functioning involves using insight and foresight to analyze and anticipate the consequences of our own actions, as well as those of others, in proactive ways to change both our own behavior and that of others so that our social environment becomes heuristically involved with our own neural development.

We can plan for the future. That ability, at its technological extreme, has made it possible for us to build weapons of mass destruction and manufacturing systems that pollute the very environment we depend on for sustenance. Now what do we do? The answer is simple, yet complex. We need to become more fully human, more aware of the often toxic consequences of our actions, through full frontal lobe development of foresight.

This is the critical difference between MacLean's evolutionary theory of the triune brain and the Qabalist point of view. MacLean—and those who assume that hominid development is merely early human development—positions the frontal lobes as an addition to the neocortex, thus chaining them to the limitations of the neocortex and to the continuity of evolution.

But what the Qabalists saw, what Jesus saw, is that the frontal lobes stand alone as a new kind of neural hardware in the brain. Jesus said, "I have meat to eat that ye know not of." Was he speaking of the substance of awareness—light—a substance that can be realized only through frontal lobe activity and which, though immaterial, provides the solidity of our authentic identity?

The frontal lobes offer us a radically different nature to identify with, a spiritual nature. Further, this new potential is based on the behavior of energy, not mass, much of which is held, like a womb, in the dark fertile possibility of intentionality. Similarly, because we are finally recognizing that the behavior of energy is full of possibilities instead of certainties, we have realized that quantum and chaos theories are unrelated to Newtonian physics. This is the nature of disruption/possibility as the opposite of continuity/certainty. Periodically, a long continuum is disrupted, birthing new potential. On this planet, we are that disruption, bursting through the evolutionary pattern with a new potentiality.

The other three cortexes are like the stepfamily in the Cinderella story, with the ugly stepsisters representing the reptilian and mammalian cortexes. The diabolical stepmother assumes the role of the neocortex, pretending to be master in the house of consciousness, enslaving Cinderella instead of freeing her. Cinderella is the same archetype as Eve. Cinderella/Eve is unrecognized, yet she represents the sweetness of transcendent human nature. It is her character that we must advance for leadership in the brain if we wish to transform and redeem the lower three cortexes in us.

Only a brain with *four* heads, the fourth being the frontal lobes, has the potential of full integration, because only through such a pattern are the frontal lobes separated, distinguished, and recognized for their distinct attributes. The new potentials in the frontal lobes offer human beings the opportunity to organize our personal and social lives—our culture—much differently from how we have in the past. For us, the new model is spiritual and transcendent, but we must identify with such traits before they will mean anything to us. Only when the full power of the prefrontal cortex is awakened can it take on the yoke of its authentic vocation, which is integrating the rest of the brain—the oldest three cortexes—into *its* advanced, angelic agenda. We must consciously integrate this new spiritual potential into our awareness if we wish it to operate in our daily lives.

Now, perhaps, you are beginning to see the brain in a new light, the light of transcendence in everyday living. That new light is made possible by a brain with four cortexes, the fourth invested with inner light. This light has also been described, in various religious and spiritual documents, as having characteristics like those of water. In Genesis, a river began as one and became four heads.

A neural description of the river in Genesis is provided by J. Scott Kelso, a neuroscientist associated with Florida-Atlantic University. He believes that new laws are necessary to describe the properties of self-organizing matter in living systems. Kelso states, in the *Brain/Mind Bulletin* of June 1996 (page 5), that the brain "... is not a box with compartments that contain sadness, joy, color, texture and all the other 'objects' and categories one might think of. Instead, I envisage it as a constantly shifting dynamic system, more like the flow of a river in which patterns emerge and disappear, than a static landscape."

Antonio Damasio and his wife, Hanna, investigate the role of emotion and memory in neural organization. Their research indicates that awareness is not due to a rigid construction of cells, but rather to a *pattern* of neural connections that has the possibility of constantly shifting, like the river Kelso describes and Genesis has immortalized.

Think of a familiar person's face. It is a memory made possible by an incredibly complex pattern of perhaps hundreds or thousands of dendritic connections. What happens if only one of the connections doesn't make it into the pattern? How does that affect the memory?

Most of us have experienced the embarrassment of seeing someone we know quite well, yet are unable to recall a name to go with the face. That part of the neural pattern didn't connect because such patterns aren't permanent. They are *reconstructed* every time we use them, like putting together a five-hundred-piece puzzle in the time it takes to blink. Moreover, the process is uniquely personal to each of us.

Memory, Damasio reminds us, is a pattern that is reconstructed every time we utilize it. The pattern is created by electrical energy that travels down neural pathways in much the same way that water travels down streambeds and river pathways. The neural pattern is created by the various connections through which the electrical energy travels during its course. Such neural patterns are always available but are by no means welded together in any permanent fashion. Neural patterns have the ability to constantly shift because of the number of connections involved in the pattern. Those connections, sometimes thousands of them, allow the pathways enormous flexibility, like a river—moving, changing course, taking the path of least resistance, which sometimes leaps out of old boundaries and forms new patterns. This flexibility is what allows periodic breakthroughs to occur.

This amazing neural river "became unto four heads," as the ancient story in Genesis narrates, because it flows through four cortexes.

COMPLETION: CONNECTING UP WHAT IS UNCONNECTED

One final piece of data MacLean imparts reveals the purpose of the hero's journey as well as the plot in Genesis. The separate cortexes, he declares, are *not* very well connected in terms of psychological integration. They behave much like separate countries within a continent, each with its own unique political, economic, and social agenda. Though we think of the brain as one unit, a convoluted mass of gray tissue, each of its four distinct and separate cortexes emerged from different phases of evolution, driven by unique survival factors.

This neural predisposition toward separation is further aggravated by tenacious cultural beliefs—religious, political, and social—that have the combined effect of maintaining our brain's psychological compartmentalization so that we remain spiritually incomplete. And therein lies the problem that cannot be addressed by any cultural means, but only by individuals as they heroically tackle the journey to awareness and wholeness. Until enough individuals travel this path, this road less traveled, enough to make up a large group that can have an effect on public policy, we will not have a movement big enough to be taken seriously. If this critical mass were to be established, the same government effort now invested in oil production and processing would be used for the development of alternative energy and for the reduction or elimination of all toxic manufacturing processes. Models for this are now emerging. One such example is a village called Las Gaviotas, on the high plains of Colombia, which is the subject of a book entitled *Gaviotas: A Village to Reinvent the World*. Lonely individuals and visionary groups are the unappreciated heroes of personal and social evolution in this all too common human saga.

One other piece of information I like to throw into this pot is the alternating pattern inherent in the four cortexes. If the Qabalic definitions for *germ* and *husk* are applied to the brain's four neural structures, and if those germinating and husking qualities are perceived as masculine (husk) and feminine (germ), an alternating pattern is perceived in cortical development: The r-complex is masculine, the limbic system is feminine, the neocortex is masculine, and the frontal lobes are feminine. The universal pattern of integrating opposites is clearly present, twice. This allows us to understand why patriarchy forms a static social pattern and why we must outgrow it and produce a social pattern that mirrors the whole-systems pattern if we wish to be fully human.

Patriarchy is invested in the two masculine cortexes, the r-complex and the neocortex, while it simultaneously devalues and diminishes the qualities of the two feminine cortexes, the limbic system and the frontal lobes. This puts us all at a disadvantage in our own development. Our most human qualities, invested in the frontal lobes, are continually and systematically denied, devalued, and diminished by the neocortex. Is it any wonder we live in a world engaged in constant battle?

The only way our world will change is if each individual outgrows the old patriarchal husk of attitudes, social values, and assumptions with which most of us have been raised. The *integration* of feminine and masculine qualities in consciousness will produce, instead, "masculine" rationale in the service of "feminine" vision, "feminine" emotions honed by "masculine" analysis, and "masculine" protection so that people and "feminine" ideas can grow unmolested. The new interpretation of Genesis offered here is merely one phase in that growth process as we nudge the brain out of its culturally inherited rigidity and into a state of fertile possibilities.

It is our lack of psychological unity that plays an enormous role, I believe, in all forms of personal and social dysfunction. Most of our problems—from an absence of simple personal happiness to alarming escalations in antisocial, criminal, and terrorist behavior—have their roots in the brain's lack of neural and psychological integration. Add to that our confusion concerning the role the frontal lobes play in human affairs and it becomes clear there is much internal work to be done if we are to successfully transform our neural pieces into a unified and whole interactive system that helps us achieve our goals of happiness, wisdom, creativity, and love.

A lack of neural integration in our own brain is something most of us rarely consider. When things go wrong in our lives, we don't usually say to ourselves, "It's those faulty synapses of mine." We don't recognize that we are functioning with an incomplete neural instrument in terms of psychological and spiritual development, that what we lack is an awareness of inner light. In order to evaluate our behavior in terms of its personal and social implications, we need to consider that the brain is unfinished until inner light is fully integrated and that our primary job as human beings is to engage in that completion process. This is our spiritual and psychological work, the journey of the soul: the process of integrating inner light into the neural fibers of the brain until wholeness is achieved. It is imperative that we recognize the situation because without that inner journey, we take life's cruise in the leakiest of neural boats.

Culture deals with our leaky neural structure by instructing us to bail frantically; we are constantly dealing with social crises because we do not understand what causes them. The most effective way to deal with such leaks, however, is simply to plug them. All spiritual adepts have seen this same problem and addressed it the same way, through varying terminologies and practices. The main point to remember is that each of us individually must learn to plug up our own leaks. No one can do it for us. To do this, it is imperative that we learn to recognize exactly where the leaks occur. It helps, therefore, to have a general understanding of the nature of neurons in the brain.

Until only a few short years ago, scientists believed that the adult brain was incapable of neural regeneration, that if you lost or damaged neurons in the brain, you were out of luck because the adult brain couldn't grow new ones. Recent studies have concluded, however, that this assumption is false; the brain does have the potential to constantly grow new neurons, not only into adulthood but even into old age as well, if we actively engage the process.

That is the hero's job in this myth: to actively undertake the process of neural generation, now appropriately termed neurogenesis, growing new linkages that integrate the four cortexes under new leadership, that of the frontal lobes. By actively seeing the inner world and its participation in the inner/outer interplay—a process made possible by the unique powers of the frontal lobes—the brain spontaneously changes. The simple act of *seeing and recognizing* germinates new neural seedlings and connections because this act involves light. Light is energy that can travel down neural pathways and even generate new neural pathways.

The light of awareness is an incredibly powerful force. It can show us the way to self-completion, to wholeness. This is not a new idea. There are two famous metaphors in the Bible, about bread and wine, that point to the critical role humans play in their own spiritual and psychological completion, which is, at its foundation, a neural evolution involving the processing of personal and social information.

Here's what I mean: No bunch of grapes could ever become wine by themselves. It takes an intervening process, humanly applied, to turn a product of nature—grapes—into wine. Likewise, no batch of wheat could ever turn itself into bread. Again, it takes a humanly applied process to transform wheat into bread, the finished product.

The brain works the same way. It cannot complete itself through nature's processes, whether evolutionary or biological, but only through an engaged process of awareness that each person must activate and which germinates new neural seedlings with an integrative intention. This, the hero's journey of the soul resulting in wholeness, is depicted in Genesis and the New Testament, as well as in familiar tales such as "The Frog Prince," "Sleeping Beauty," and "Beauty and the Beast."

The process of psychological completion involves actively hooking up compartmentalized and fragmented elements in the brain, including the separate cortexes, by growing and weaving new neural channels among them. Neurogenesis is stimulated by the perception and recognition of the activities of the inner world and how they interact with activities in the outer world: the personal and social dimensions of intelligence. This neural integration occurs through potentials that we commonly refer to as intuition, insight, foresight, and awareness, by which we gather information using light. The frontal lobes are in charge here, represented by Eve in her relationship with Adam and by Beauty as she tames the Beast.

The juice that inspires all this inner activity is desire. We must desire wholeness in order to construct it so we can experience it. Desire, in this sense, is intentionality. This is how we plug up our neural leaks: not by seeking help from God, but by doing our own internal work so we can realize the power of light within us, in our angelic frontal lobes.

There are all sorts of techniques for seeing the interplay between the outer and inner worlds, and for recording what we see. Some people write in journals. Some paint, sing, or dance. Others shape clay or make dolls or puppets or form theater groups. Some meditate, while others jog. The method isn't important; it's the journey of growth that matters. Growth and fertilization are the natural result of recognizing the inner/outer interplay.

The reason the prefrontal cortex administrates this area of our life is that it is the only cortex capable of looking inward to the interior of the brain itself, where the mysteries of the self, soul, and spirit—our inner light—await our investigation. The function of looking inward is characterized by terms such as *self-awareness, self-examination,* and *higher consciousness,* which, the Qabalists insisted, are not "higher" functions, but rather the only authentic level of functioning available for human beings because it emanates from the frontal lobes. The term *higher consciousness,* then, refers to the "higher" awareness of the frontal lobes.

Self-awareness is synonymous with brain awareness and leads to neural integration. It includes many activities and potentials based on one function: seeing inward, the function of insight. Quantum scientists have proved that the mere observation of photons changes their direction. The same principle applies to the brain. Self-observation and self-examination can change the direction of neural connections. When that change occurs, our thinking instantaneously leaps "out of the box." A man in prison, with no other skills or education, changed his life merely by observing and scrutinizing his own feelings and memories of his social interactions with his father, which amounted to engaging the personal and social dimensions of intelligence. Looking inward changed the direction of neural connections in his brain, allowing him to peer outside the box he was raised in and see himself with new eyes, which is transcendence. Looking inward, through insight harnessed to recognition, has the power to change, alter, and transform the neural networks in the brain, and *that* can change the way we see everything else. Everything.

Neuroscientist Elkhonon Goldberg points out, in *The Executive Brain: Frontal Lobes and the Civilized Mind* (Oxford University Press, 2001), that the frontal lobes are associated with the mysterious power of intentionality. The Qabalists insisted that first and foremost we should use this power of intentionality to answer the deep call of our soul for integration. In the New Testament a primary message is "Seek ye *first* the kingdom of heaven . . ." This first vocation—personal (neural) integration—is achieved through our intentionality invested in the frontal lobes, because intentionality is germ energy, the power we call on when we want to engender a new pattern, a new business, a new attitude, a new way of being. Intentionality, in short, is the power of genesis.

Unfortunately, the priority of our intentions is often organized, not by the frontal lobes, but by the rational qualities invested in the neocortex. In our culture, an intention of spirituality and integration is often subordinated to the *perceived* needs of the neocortex and its focus on survival, and especially on surviving well—with money, degrees, power, fame, and so forth. Survival needs are important, there's no doubt about that, but when such needs subordinate our equally important spiritual needs, balance and wholeness are sacrificed. In that case we may survive, and sometimes very well, but we will not be happy.

The neocortex often assumes the role of authority in the brain because it has become the most developed through the last three thousand years of cultural education. It has benefited from the curriculum of symbol processing in reading, writing, arithmetic, and technological advancement, which is symbolized by the seventh day in Genesis. The authoritarian overtones of the neocortex, however, make it a bad master, especially when dealing with the deep intentions of the soul. Consequently, we spend much of our lives confused about what we really want. We devote years to achieving certain successes only to discover we are not fulfilled by them the way we imagined we would be. A character in an old romance novel I read a decade ago put it this way, "I jist cain't figure out why I ain't as happy as I wanna be."

One of the best ways to circumvent the neocortex's assumed authority in our lives is to associate our identity with the frontal lobes. One of the major points the Qabalists recognized through the actions of Eve in Genesis is that the frontal lobes are the most advanced cortex in the brain, containing the most advanced agenda—neural integration. The Qabalah understands that identifying with the spiritual and psychological agenda of the prefrontal cortex empowers its intentionality for integration. This is what Adam does in the Genesis story, although it isn't easy for him.

In the Old Testament, the Burning Bush that Moses encountered says, "I am that I am." Is this not how we identify ourselves? *I am.* The bush said, "Tell them *I am* has sent you." It was the voice of the frontal lobes, the only cortex in the brain that is fully human, and can therefore *claim* our authentic identity.

Neural integration is the intention of our soul, our *I am,* and often gestates astonishing and surprising results. Those results are often scoffed at by our rational mind, or even outright denied when they present themselves in the form of psychic powers, synchronistic events, transcendent experiences, or mystical visions. Many of us have had such experiences, 70 percent by one count, and science is now attempting to embrace such experiences as legitimate subjects for study. These potentials represent the sparkling jewels in Eve's dowry, bequeathed to each of us and illumined with cosmic light.

Lorenzo's Oil is a movie based on the true story of a young boy, Lorenzo, afflicted with a rare disorder that medical science knows very little about. His parents, though they have no medical background, are determined to heal their son. They empower their intentions by devoting their lives to researching enormous amounts of medical data in the hope that something has been overlooked. Then one night, after years of heartache and at the point of exhaustion, the boy's father has a dream that gives him critical clues about how certain cells are malfunctioning in his son's body. By enlisting the help of scientists in creating a formula, Lorenzo's parents do what all the medical professionals researching his disorder have failed to do: They miraculously find the cure in a simple chemical procedure involving olive oil, hence the title of the film.

Intentionality gives Lorenzo's parents the drive and insights that eventually produce the result they are after, a result that had never existed previously, a result that is snatched from the void of the unknown. That result originates in a dream, which some scientists say should not be trusted as a source of information. But the results in Lorenzo's situation are conclusive. The dream contains information that is as trustworthy as the fact that Earth orbits the sun. It is a dream that originates within the psyche of Lorenzo's father, inspired by his intention to find a cure for his son. Such intentions have enormous power. Jesus spoke of them when he said, "Blessed are the pure in heart, for they shall see God." Notice that he didn't say, "Blessed are the pious" or "Blessed are the devoted." He said, "Blessed are the pure in heart" because he was referring to internal states of pure intentionality.

The frontal lobes are gifted with amazing powers, and it is these gifts that are essential to our uniqueness as human beings. Intentionality is what allows us to change ourselves and our world. It is the juice of creativity. Empowered with the amazing force of intentionality, the prefrontal cortex allows breakthroughs to occur from the unknown.

Breakthroughs are often perceived as miraculous or extraordinary, yet are they not often the result of employing intentionality to discover one's purest desire? The father *wanted* to cure Lorenzo.

The prefrontal cortex, because of this remarkable power of intention, does not resemble the other cortexes. It is not directed by the evolutionary imperatives for sensory perception that drove the development of the r-complex, limbic system, and neocortex. Instead it represents a new agenda of transformative possibility and transcendent potential.

The rational intellect is the worst possible intelligence to be charged with naming and defining the attributes of the frontal lobes because after three thousand years of academics devoted to studies concerning the outer world, it doesn't in the least understand the inner potentiality of the prefrontal cortex. Unless the intellect has been prepared, it does not know how to approach the intuitive, synchronistic, and insightful characteristics that endow the frontal lobes. Such *nonrational* attributes are outside the box of its conditioned thinking, so it often dismisses evidence of their performance without investigation.

Dr. Goldberg brings up another situation that points to the inability of rationale to deal with the possibilities of the frontal lobes. He relates the research of Allan Shore, a psychiatrist from Southern California, who posits that early mother-infant interaction is important for normal development of the orbitofrontal cortex, a portion of the frontal lobes, during the first months of life. If this is true, Dr. Goldberg states, it would be mind-boggling, because it implies that early social interaction helps shape the brain. But why should such a hypothesis be mind-boggling? Obviously the idea that the brain is shaped in part by early social interaction between mother and infant is mind-boggling only to a rationale that has previously assumed it wasn't.

An intellect assumes such interaction does not shape the brain because it doesn't see the pattern that may prove that it does. That doesn't mean the pattern isn't there. It means the intellect doesn't *see* the pattern and therefore leaps to the assumption that one doesn't exist. This suggests a major point of the Genesis myth: We have to open our eyes, remove the logs of assumption that blind us to ourselves and especially to the special powers of the frontal lobes. The intellect often makes blind assumptions and if those blind assumptions are made by a high enough authority, the rest of us often believe them, even if they are dead wrong.

Discovering truth is an essential part of the journey to wholeness. We often act on assumptions as if they were truths—for example, defining a tree's fruit as the knowledge of good and evil and then assuming all women should be devalued because a religious authority has told us it was a woman who, in eating the fruit of the tree, disobeyed the commandment not to eat it. The fact that she was never given the commandment in the first place, which can be determined from a literal reading of the text, seems to have escaped them.

The prefrontal cortex is the neural structure that looks inward, where *all* our assumptions are made. Looking inward with the intention of seeing the truth offers the possibility of uncovering (or betraying) the intellect's errors and assumptions. This is the most difficult task we will ever undertake because we are often heavily invested in those errors, so much so that we would rather go to war than change them, as the Confederacy did to protect its "rights" concerning slavery, and that we seem determined to do today to protect our interests in foreign oil. The intellect often hinders and blocks the very information that intention desires because it is invested in maintaining a status quo of sacred cows rather than in searching for new truths.

Such intellectual resistance must be overcome in order for us to contact, or transcend to, the unknown, where a new fecundity of mind awaits our discovery. Firmly attached to what is known or often merely assumed, the intellect is sometimes the biggest obstacle on the hero's journey into the unknown of the soul's desire. If the resistance of the rational intellect cannot be overcome, the unknown cannot be contacted and the elixir, the "Lorenzo's oil," or the knowledge of wholeness, cannot be retrieved.

The transcendent breakthrough of intentionality over a resisting intellect is represented by an act of betrayal in a few famous biblical metaphors, such as the betrayal of Jesus' intellect so that the resurrection could occur and the betrayal of Joseph's intellect so that his dreaming powers could be used to predict the future and eventually lead to the freeing of the Hebrews. Judas and Joseph's brothers are elements of Jesus' and Joseph's psyches, respectively. Betraying the intellect (and its resistance to unknown possibilities) allows the prefrontal cortex to break into a deep vault of unrecognized potential in order to retrieve the elixir it desires—which in this story is the wisdom desired by Eve—bringing with it the information of wholeness and integration.

The purpose of mythology is to produce this betrayal, to bypass the intellect by telling a story that is so compelling that the intellect becomes entranced. In this way the message of the myth is delivered to the psyche without the intellect's resistance intruding with thoughts such as "That's impossible!" or "It defies the laws of logic and reality!" which stop the investigation before it even begins. A story about a woman who talks to a serpent, desires wisdom, then eats a fruit that opens her eyes is precisely such a tale.

The unknown includes our transcendent level of functioning, our spirituality. A good way to recognize that this functioning is easily dismissed by the intellect of the neocortex is to note that spirituality is seldom taught as a subject in schools, colleges, or universities. Religion is often taught, but not spirituality. It is, however, a booming subject in the literary field, where millions of books are bought each year by individuals seeking such knowledge. What they are really seeking is information about the transcendent and transformative behavior and potential contained within the frontal lobes, activated through intentionality.

Through intent, intuition, and insight, the frontal lobes are often in contact with those possibilities waiting in the unknown that the intellect, controlled by the forces of certainty, insists cannot be there. The frontal lobes are somehow aware of possibilities and events that can happen at any moment, circumstances that seem to be lined up just so. Somehow, inexplicably, the prefrontal cortex nudges us to intuitive action: to buy a book we hadn't intended, to call someone we don't ordinarily socialize with, to seek advice we hadn't previously allowed, to explore an area we had originally dismissed. Sometimes, in order to nudge us into this action, we have to quiet the neocortex's resistance and often the results of our intuitive action are mysteriously successful. Amazingly, when we embark upon a hero's journey to wholeness, it seems as though the universe is in sync with us, providing whatever we need along the way. Perhaps the neurochemistry of intentionality "softens" the brain in a way that helps us recognize things we normally wouldn't, opening us to possibilities we haven't previously seen or considered. Lorenzo's father had a dream that he couldn't dismiss.

The portion of the brain that produces this special neurochemistry, allowing us to perceive the seed of possibilities in the unknown and steer us in that direction, is the prefrontal cortex, its buried light acting as intuition, insight, and foresight, which we often refer to as hunches or gut feelings or flashes of inspiration. She is who we are about to meet in Genesis and it is she who directs the heroic inner journey into the unknown of the brain and psyche, recovering the elixir of the knowledge of wholeness that leads to clarity.

4

Adam's Directives and Helpmate: The Neocortex and the Frontal Lobes

A hero's journey always consists of difficult tasks to be performed or enormous obstacles to be overcome. In Genesis the hero's task is to discover, recognize, and then construct a whole system of awareness from the fragmented, compartmentalized, and alienated elements of the patriarchal brain and psyche, in which the intellect has unwittingly become a major contributor to incompleteness and rigidity of thought. It is, indeed, a hero's task.

When most of us think of the brain, what we are usually thinking of is its formidable intellect, the cognitive power of the neocortex. However, as we have seen, we possess other vital forms of intelligence that are often discounted by the intellect. The aspect of intelligence that plays the most important role in terms of integration—the prefrontal cortex—is represented in Genesis by the image of Eve. Offering a perfect example of how the intellect often devalues other forms of intelligence, Eve is traditionally perceived as the original "fallen woman," alone responsible for the sinful state of the human race.

A major goal of the hero's journey in Genesis is to reeducate the intellect so it can perceive the brain's other forms of intelligence with more respect and appreciation, especially that represented by Eve. The prefrontal cortex is a major influence in reorienting the intellect so it can be a better conduit for information, especially the information of new possibilities. In its present state, the intellect generally operates under the influence of cultural biases that in a patriarchal society work to support the status quo, thus limiting the brain's innate fertility and flexibility.

Status quo thinking, based on Newtonian certainties, has been culturally indoctrinated into the rational intellect through our academic institutions. With the advent of quantum and chaos theories, and new models of whole systems, such paradigms of certainty are no longer the only choices for interpreting information or events, especially the mythological and psychological events we are investigating here.

In order for us to accomplish the task of fertilizing the intellect with new life, we must put it through a rigorous reeducation process, a psychological boot camp. That process prepares its symbolic thinking apparatus to expand beyond the rigidities imposed by cultural paradigms of certainty so it can recognize the importance of new possibilities and opportunities. A major outgrowth of this process is that the intellect finally learns to recognize its authentic position within the brain's hierarchy of cortexes, which may come as either a shock or a surprise, depending on your point of view.

The first step of our journey, therefore, is recognition. We need to recognize that the parts of our neural instrument are just that, parts. There is no whole unless and until we build the neural and psychological connections that integrate those parts, which is a major portion of the hero's assignment being described in the Genesis myth. The role of the frontal lobes, when recognized properly by the neocortex—the cortex that names and defines—is to instigate that psychological linkage, because it is the frontal lobes that are invested with intention. When our intention is to become whole, it is the frontal lobes that are called into service.

The fact that our spirit, soul, and psyche have an actual home in the frontal lobes of the brain is the remarkable knowledge of the Genesis myth. It means that we don't need to go to any special place to find this home, not to church or synagogue or mosque. We don't need to be anointed or baptized by any outside authority. All we need to do is turn inward. This *inward* dimension is often characterized by feminine qualities just as the *outer* dimension is characterized as masculine, following the universal pattern inherent in germ and husk: interior and exterior. In the brain and psyche, the frontal lobes—Eve—process the information of the inner world while the neocortex—Adam—processes information from the outer world.

In Genesis 2 Adam is given four directives to promote the intentions of wholeness. They change his character, shaping and kneading more flexibility into his awareness, reducing his tendencies toward egoistic certainties, until he can finally cleave unto the one who is his salvation, the frontal lobes. The first directive occurs in Genesis 2:15 when man is put into the garden to "dress" and "keep" it. The second is a commandment so famous it hardly needs mentioning: He is restricted, in Genesis 2:17, from eating the fruit of the tree of the knowledge of good and evil. Verses twenty through twenty-three contain the third directive, indicating that he is supposed to find and name his helpmate. Finally, in Genesis 2:24, he is directed to cleave unto his wife. These four directives, when understood mythologically, evolve the intellect's symbolic thinking processes, expanding its choices for interpretation and inspiring its vision with new possibilities, new horizons, and new fecundity.

As we have learned, according to the mythology and cosmology of Qabalah, inner is feminine, characterized by germ energy, and outer is masculine, characterized by husk energy. In the human psyche, germ energy must be allowed the freedom it requires in order to keep growing. The pattern of patriarchy, however, devalues all things feminine, including the inner world, which responds by shutting down. This is why Adam needs to be rescued. He needs the inner world to be fully alive in order to claim his authentic humanity.

Adam—meaning the patriarchal, monotheistic, and misogynist intellect—has become static and rigid. The tree of the knowledge of good and evil is *his* tree because his paradigms have defined it. Astonishingly, he has absolutely no idea what he has wrought with those definitions, namely the static state of his own mind. He needs some help and this story provides it through the image of the helpmate. Eve is the only one who can alter and expand his interpretive limitations because she is his opposite, the feminine. It is important to note that she does not yet exist in the story when Adam is restricted from eating the fruit of the tree of good and evil, and this may be *why* the commandment is given. Adam needs her disruptive perspective in order to shatter his own static perceptions and create an opportunity for germination of thought to occur.

Patriarchal structures in the psyche, especially in the psyches of men, build resistances that shut down the ability to pay attention to activities taking place in the inner world. Eve cannot rescue Adam until those resistances are lowered, until Adam becomes humble and receptive. Patriarchy puts men in the narcissistic position of thinking they don't need to be rescued, so Adam must be coaxed into humility. He is given the four directives so that he can gain a new orientation, one that is more flexible and less rigid. Each of the directives helps him move *away* from his old habits of certainty in Newtonian thinking and *toward* the unknown potentials and possibilities of transcendent clarity offered by the prefrontal cortex, until he finally "cleaves" unto her at the end of Genesis 2.

THE FIRST DIRECTIVE

Immediately following the verses describing the four rivers that began as one (representing the four cortexes), the man in Genesis (who will later be named Adam) is put into the garden and given his first directive.

> *And the Lord God took the man and*
> *put him into the garden of Eden to*
> *dress it and keep it.*
>
> GENESIS 2:15

Usually considered merely poetic by traditional interpretations, this verse, upon further investigation, offers vital clues concerning the intellect's role within the garden. If the words *dress* and *keep* are translated back into Hebrew using Strong's *Concordance,* they reveal something interesting about the intellect. "To dress" is *Abad,* which means "to work and to till" but also "to enslave." "To keep" is *Shamar,* which means "to hedge about with thorns," "to guard," "to protect," "to beware." (The thorns remind me of the crown of thorns worn by Jesus.) These definitions reveal characteristics of the intellect that aren't often discussed. They refer to its capacity to prick and poke the mind, leaving holes and gaps that often enlarge into deception, delusion, fabrication, and assumption, tying us up in knots—enslaving us—to our own thoughts, analyses, and paradigms, even when we know they are dead wrong. Cigarette manufacturers arguing in Congress that they hadn't known nicotine is addictive or lumber companies arguing that clear-cutting is good for the environment illustrate perfectly this mechanism. The intellect is often a cunning, cold-hearted tyrant in its quest to further its own agenda of continuity and authority. Today the internal combustion engine is under attack because it causes so much air pollution, yet car manufacturers fight aggressively to maintain their status quo, even though cleaner emission engines are easily manufactured.

The Qabalists understood all too well the intellect's stubbornness and shortsightedness because they were aware of how the forces of certainty and continuity—already established in the brain and in patriarchal culture's hierarchies of power—work to maintain an intellectual status quo and prevent spiritual, psychological, and even intellectual innovation. Therefore, they put the man in the garden to dress it and keep it, to work it or be enslaved by it, to take heed and beware of it.

The Qabalists were intimately aware of the intellect's prickly behavior in this regard. Other students of wisdom have noted it too. Historian and Pulitzer Prize–winner Daniel J. Boorstin, now Librarian of Congress emeritus, is recognized for his ability to condense a whole society, many societies in fact, into a few simple themes. From science to farming, Boorstin views Western history as a battle between innovators and bureaucrats, those who think for themselves and those who let others think for them. In this, he proves to be a first-class Qabalic thinker. He recognizes that innovators use foresight and intentionality (located in the frontal lobes), while bureaucrats are those stuck in rationale, using the neocortex's fomidable intellectual powers as a bully pulpit to maintain the status quo and thus their social power base.

As most of us know, innovators such as Galileo, Margaret Sanger, Martin Luther King Jr., Nelson Mandela, and a league of others too numerous to mention have often been harassed, ridiculed, imprisoned, or even murdered by bureaucrats and those who thought in step with them. Yet it is the innovators among us who provide the juice for progress. That powerful juice, I propose, originates in the frontal lobes with their potentialities of insight, foresight, intuition, and intentionality.

The intellect often clings ferociously to the certainty of the known, stealing the thunder of the prefrontal cortex by simply invalidating her agenda. Such a mind is often obsessed with scientific facts, yet is devoid of the knowledge and power of intention in spirit and soul. Isn't this the mind, at least in most Western societies, in control of public policy? The r-complex (reptilian) and the neocortex (hominid/intellect) behave, in many ways, as brothers in crime. When their energies and activities haven't been integrated properly, when their power has not been tempered by whole-systems awareness and the vital function of intentionality, they often run fast and loose together to block change. They formulate paradigms such as slavery and the flat Earth, and use positions of power and authority to dominate and intimidate others, maintaining a status quo that, even now, continues to destroy the natural environment around us. Because of this, the next verses, which issue the second directive to Adam, are almost self-explanatory.

THE SECOND DIRECTIVE

And the Lord God commanded the
man, saying, Of every tree of the
garden thou mayest freely eat:

But of the tree of the knowledge of
good and evil, thou shalt not eat
of it: for in the day that thou eatest
thereof thou shalt surely die.

GENESIS 2:16–17

Here we arrive at one of the major imperatives driving the Genesis story. The man—the patriarchal intellect—is forbidden to eat the fruit of the tree of the knowledge of good and evil. This commandment is so indelibly etched in our minds that almost all of us in Western civilization know it, whether we've read the Bible or not. Our cultural landscape is strewn with its memory. If the man eats that fruit, he will die.

This is why it is interesting to notice that the woman does not yet exist in the story. Only the man exists at this point, in the garden, receiving this commandment. *She* is not ever given the commandment, yet for three thousand years she has been heaped with blame for disobeying it. It is also interesting to note that when the man finally does eat the fruit later in the story, *after* she eats it first, he doesn't die. In fact, neither of them dies. Something entirely different and wonderful happens instead.

After they eat the fruit, their eyes are opened. Now, obviously their eyes had been open before, so what kind of new eyes are these that are opening?

Traditional interpretations view the eating of that eye-opening fruit as the entire downfall of humanity, and blame it entirely on the woman. Yet what is so horrible about eating a fruit that opens your eyes? Where is the evil in that? The traditional interpretation of this story is a perfect example of the abusive authority and misguided assumptions of the neocortex because it cannot logically comprehend it. Only *mytho-logic* can understand this story, which requires a different kind of thinking, a new way of seeing.

According to the mythology of the Qabalists, this man, the patriarchal intellect, is forbidden the fruit of the tree of the knowledge of good and evil because of what he would do with it in his present state of *assumed* authority, which is pretty much what he actually *has* done with it. A compartmentalized, fragmented, enslaved-to-the-known intellect is unable to perceive the psychological ramifications of its own short-sighted definitions of the words *good* and *evil*. Such an intellect must be restricted from even exploring such powerful and corruptible knowledge until it has built a foundation of awareness capable of integrating it within a whole-systems perspective. In order to do that, the intellect must be firmly attached to the one neural structure in the brain that can provide such a foundation, the frontal lobes, represented by Eve. After the restriction from eating the fruit is placed, therefore, the very next event is the preparation for that all-important connection.

> *And the Lord God said, It is not good*
> *that the man should be alone: I will*
> *make him an helpmate for him.*
>
> GENESIS 2:18

Much has been assumed by traditional interpreters concerning the desirable duties this helpmate should provide. She has been glorified because her sole job, as they have seen it, is to help and please man. A helpmate is supposed to cook his meals, wash his clothes, keep his house, discipline his children, and obey his every whim. It is the patriarchal dream.

Only thing is, *this* helpmate never does any of those things in *this* story. So much for assumptions. This helpmate offers only one kind of help: eating the forbidden fruit *without* dying. Remember, the commandment said that the man was forbidden to eat the fruit because he would die. So what kind of magic does the woman possess that enables her to eat that fruit and still live and also to pass such a desirable trait to the man? For not only do both of them live, but they live with new eyes, eyes that are now open with a new fertility and fecundity.

THE THIRD DIRECTIVE

In the next two verses, immediately after the helpmate is mentioned, two curious things happen.

> *And out of Adamah [ground] the Lord God*
> *formed every beast of the field, and*
> *every fowl of the air; and brought them*
> *unto Adam to see what he would call*
> *them: and whatsoever Adam called*
> *every living creature, that was the*
> *name thereof.*
>
> *And Adam gave names to all cattle,*
> *and to the fowl of the air, and to every*
> *beast of the field; but for Adam there*
> *was not found an helpmate for him.*
>
> GENESIS 2:19–20

First, the man receives his name in the very same verse in which he is ordered to name all the animals. Isn't that an interesting coincidence? Or is it a Qabalic clue? Notice how all those animals spring from Adamah, "the ground." Adamah, as we have seen, is the fertilized matter of the brain that generates the neural networks producing awareness. In this case, the man must name the animals as he simultaneously receives his own name. Yet that name is not given to him in any ceremonial way; it simply happens because that is part of his self-definition process.

This man, now named Adam, is the neocortical intellect, placed in the garden of awareness to "dress it and keep it," meaning to work it and beware of it so as not to be enslaved by its errors and assumptions. He is also forbidden the fruit of the infamous tree. Now he needs a helpmate so he won't be alone. It doesn't say he needs a helpmate to be his slave, serving his every need. It says he needs a helpmate so he won't be *alone,* without relationship, because relationship offers him the fundamentals of all whole systems, an integration of opposites. But in the next verse, instead of the appearance of the helpmate, what happens? He gets a name and is ordered to name a bunch of animals. What a curious riddle. Yet when knowledge of the brain and Western cultural patterns are revealed, they perfectly match the state of male self-awareness, a condition that is ubiquitous throughout Western civilization, even three thousand years after the myth was written. We are still living in the symbolic seventh day of patriarchal symbol processing in the brain and have not yet transcended our own limiting self-definitions. Cultural man with his cultural intellect, to whom this portion of the text is directed, has no idea who or what his helpmate is, or why he needs her, so first he must get a little education. He is ordered to name the animals. Why? Because naming is what the intellect does. Consider the entire scientific process that commonly uses Latin to name new species of animals and plants. Naming defines a specific attribute of intellectual activity. Defining the world around us helps us organize awareness and become knowledgeable. Naming is the quintessential activity of the human intellect in this seventh-day cycle of symbol processing.

But there's a question these verses point to that goes unrecognized. If naming defines, how do we then name and define ourselves? Throughout Western literature there is an awareness that we humans do not know how to properly identify and define ourselves or our behavior. We are a mystery unto ourselves. Science abounds with information and knowledge about the outer world: the environment, geology, astronomy, and so forth. But clear knowledge about human identity and behavior is up for grabs. This is part of what's being addressed here. It begins with Adam naming the animals.

The beasts are paraded before Adam, who finally has his own name, which in turn helps him name the animals and therefore organize his awareness. This is a metaphor that depicts the intellect developing, educating, and organizing itself, honing its skills and evolving its structure. It is more or less the process that Western civilization has been engaged in for the past three thousand years through the symbol processing involved in literacy and academic education. When we go to school, this type of education is what we receive. Name things, name everything, name the alphabet, the parts of a sentence, the parts of a cell, the parts of the body, the events in history, the names of the presidents, and so forth. Yet even though the intellect has accomplished all that, it still can't find its helpmate. It is still alone, without any authentic spiritual guidance, because the cortex that provides it has not yet been located and recognized.

SOLVING THE RIDDLES

There is a riddle here in Genesis, if you know how to read the Qabalic code. In the narration of the evolutionary events leading to human creation in Genesis 1:27, the words used are ". . . male and female created he them." Most of us are familiar with these words, but the Qabalic version offers a much deeper picture.

Qabalah—transcending the mind's symbol-processing skills beyond cultural levels to cosmic awareness—can be studied using either letters or numbers. Each letter has a corresponding number. In addition to being read as acronyms, the words of text in Genesis can also be read as *number formulas*. For example, Aleph, which is the intermittent spark without which nothing is, can also be symbolized using the number 1. Bayt, which is the archetype of containers, or dwellings, is also symbolized by the number 2. There is no zero. The numbers of Qabalah go from 1 to 9, from 10 to 90, and from 100 to 900 (see appendix 1). If we look at the word *man* in Genesis 1:27 and then look at *helpmate,* a startling situation is revealed. *Man* is ZAKAR, 7.20.200, Zayn (7), Kaf (20), Raysh (200) (see appendix 1). Zayn is indeterminate fertility in form, Kaf is a biologic container, and Raysh is the cosmic container. ZAKAR means that the indeterminate potential of 7 is encased within two containers.

Helpmate is EZER, Ayn (70), Zayn (7), Raysh (200). ZAKAR/*man* is 7.20.200. Ezer/*helpmate* is 70.7.200. Do you see how similar and yet different they are, numerically? This difference is the clue to their identities.

By deciphering the coded letters of EZER, we discover what kind of *helpmate* she is. She is 70.7.200: all possible possibilities (7) in individual form (70), carried in a universal pattern (200). Her potentiality is not encased, but rather available for use (see appendix 1). The character of Ezer is an intuitional and insightful intelligence that opposes the rational, compartmentalized intellect, which is encased in the Newtonian logic of certainty.

To gain some insight into the meaning of these numbers, we can look to the rabbinic tradition. There, a man's wife is meant to oppose him, as the germ opposes the husk, because this is what will actually make him wise. The obedient wife, the wife of patriarchy—the one who fundamentalist authorities admonish women to become, who is told to support her husband and stand by him no matter what—this wife makes her husband into a weak, arrogant fool. A man who has only an obedient wife is a man who will never grow up. He will always remain a "little dictator" because he has no one to question him, to oppose him.

The authors of Genesis are trying to tell us something important about the psyche, the cultural intellect, and the brain itself. They are saying that the rationale and logic of the intellect, useful attributes though they may be, need another, opposing form of intelligence so the intellect won't be alone in its compartmentalized logic and rational assumptions. In order to find his helpmate, however, Adam needs to recognize her specific attributes and potential as *opposite* his. This is not an easy task for him to accomplish. His patriarchal orientation does not allow him to *value* his opposite, the feminine, and it is psychologically difficult to recognize something that is not valued.

Remember Rob Hanford's thesis? A thing is important only if it matters; then we recognize its value and worth. If we assume it isn't important, or that it doesn't matter, we cannot perceive its value. Patriarchy, for three thousand years, has failed to value the contribution of women in society. Its *his*tory is a testament to that pattern. This failure to recognize is being addressed here, because Adam can't find his helpmate, which, paradoxically, is why he needs to have his eyes opened and why it is the woman who provides him this opportunity.

Immediately following the statement about Adam needing a helpmate, all the animals are produced for Adam to name and define. It is interesting to note that the animals are organized in three categories: the fowl of the air, the cattle, and the beast of the field. Could these three categories correspond to the oldest three cortexes in the human brain, which constitute Adam's evolutionary heritage? Let's investigate.

Birds are theorized as descending from dinosaurs, which were reptiles (feathers evolved from scales), and could therefore be representative of the r-complex. Cattle are mammals, which could represent the limbic system, or old mammalian brain. The "beast of the field" could be the hominids, representing the neocortex, that portion of the brain that ballooned during hominid evolution, when the beasts we now call apes climbed down from the trees and began living on the savannah, the great "fields" of Africa.

Adam could be looking at his own evolutionary trajectory and naming the elements of his own inherited neurology—the r-complex, limbic system, and neocortex—those portions of the brain that were produced during the terrestrial continuum of sensory development. Naming them separates, distinguishes, and differentiates certain elements of the psyche, those accumulated from the past. But it still doesn't help him find his helpmate, the insightful, intentional intelligence of the prefrontal cortex that will activate his future. Another theme in these verses is the search for an authentic human identity, because the prefrontal cortex—the one he can't find—contains it. Adam can't find his helpmate, so he can't recognize who he is. These verses are portraying the huge identity crisis that plagues Western man's philosophers: Who are we and why are we here?

Who Is the Helpmate? = Who Am I?

Adam's helpmate—his authentic human identity—is not discovered among those animals, not in his, or our, past. This leads to an interesting observation. Every few years or so the headlines ring with yet another discovery by a paleoanthropologist of an ancient set of hominid bones somewhere in Africa that supposedly pushes back the origins of humanity. Why? Because those scientists, like Adam, like most culturally trained thinkers, keep looking to the past for our identity, for that's how continuity operates on the intellect. And just like Adam, they aren't going to find it there.

We—the transcendent portion of us represented by the frontal lobes—are not from the past. This is what the creationists have misunderstood. In their view, humanity is a new creature, unconnected to evolutionary patterns. Sadly, they still do not recognize what makes us new, namely our intentional and transcendent potentials located in the frontal lobes, which *we* (not God) must develop in this seventh day of symbol processing because they are part of our self-discovery.

The authors of Genesis are saying something incredibly profound, which has not been understood. Humanity's identity, secretly encapsulated within the frontal lobes, being defined here as a helpmate (Ezer), is not based on what we have been, or where we have come from, or what we have accomplished in the past, but rather on what we will *yet become* by developing and activating the spiritual and visionary potentials in the frontal lobes. We are meant to transcend the past and create a new future, one that is not in continuity with the past but is instead a new vision altogether, based on the cosmic pattern of wholeness.

We are, in that sense, possibilities waiting to happen, potential expecting to be stirred into life, wet clay yearning to be shaped and formed. We are the creators of ourselves, who must ignite our own extraordinary potentials into a fertile life. We do this by recognizing the pattern of wholeness as an interplay of opposites. Adam is being called on, in these verses, to name his opposite so as to engage in that interplay. But he can't find her yet because he is still looking through eyes of continuity and certainty. He is unable, at this moment, to see (and name) his own possibilities: Ezer.

Looking through such eyes, we are as astonished today at our transcendent and transformative abilities and potentialities as anyone who has ever thought about them. Such attributes as intuition, insight, foresight, intention, and transcendence are not part of our evolutionary heritage, nor are they valued by our logical intellect or academic institutions. We do not understand why we have such potentialities because we keep trying to define them according to evolutionary theories based on paradigms of survival of the fittest and Newtonian principles. Such views completely overlook the possibilities of germ energy in the self. This is where our authentic identity lies, along with our future. Jesus said we should let children be our guide. Perhaps he was referring to the imaginative nature of children. Isn't imagination the birthing place of all new frontiers? I believe the frontal lobes play an enormous role in imagination, especially when imagination is used to solve problems.

Two women involved in social work in the Los Angeles area demonstrate this. One woman worked with gang members serving time in juvenile facilities, another woman worked with children who had physical disabilities. Both were faced with severe staff shortages. One of them had the brilliant idea to pool their resources. Why not introduce the juvenile offenders to the handicapped kids and see what could be made of it? Despite resistance from superiors and department heads, the go-ahead was given, and the project was a resounding success. The ex–gang members discovered a new purpose for living in helping the handicapped kids simply move around in physical space, and the handicapped kids found new, attentive friends. It was a perfect integration of needs and services and demonstrates that imagination and problem solving offer us many possibilities. It was the intent of the women to solve their problem that helped them discover their solution. That intent was made possible by frontal lobe activity.

The prefrontal cortex was the last neural substrate to emerge in the human brain. That makes her potentially the most complex and the most advanced neural tissue available. However, she remains unrecognized by the neocortex, which keeps her from being fully activated.

This, I believe, is our biggest problem, the so-called human problem: We do not recognize that the frontal lobes contain our identity. And in this lack of recognition, the neocortex has stolen the thunder of the frontal lobes. We all pay dearly for it. This is Adam's plight, as well as our own. He is stuck in a failure-to-recognize quagmire. He desperately needs some help.

The authors of Genesis intervene, therefore, in the same way life often intervenes when we need help but don't know it. Think about it. What often happens to us when we are humming along in our continuous mode of certainty, keeping up with the Joneses, but not paying attention to our inner life, to our soul's intentions? Wham! Something comes along and metaphorically thunks us on the head with a proverbial two-by-four. A car accident, cancer, loss of a loved one, a financial crisis, or some other (perceived) catastrophe is life's way of getting our attention in order to remind us of what is important about living. Just so, Adam is knocked unconscious in Genesis. He is put to sleep. When he wakes up, everything will be different, because now what's important will be right before his eyes, where he can't miss it. And he will finally recognize it. Sort of.

WAKING UP

And the Lord God caused a deep sleep
to fall upon Adam, and he slept: and
he took one of his ribs, and closed
up the flesh instead thereof . . .

GENESIS 2:21

In Hebrew, the "deep sleep," is *Tardamah Yashen*. Tardamah is Tav-Raysh-Dallet-Mem (400.200.4.40). Tav is the total resistance of life's physical support and Raysh is the total organic process of universal life. *Dam* (which derives from Dallet-Mem) is "blood." *Damah* is the feminine of blood. Adam, Aleph-Dallet-Mem, means "Aleph in the Blood." Here, in this verse, Adam's blood is being (deeply) fertilized by a feminine quality while he is Yashen (asleep), from a primitive root meaning "to be slack or languid." Such a state is the opposite of the often rigid, intellectual attitudes of society's authority figures. In this slack, relaxed state, like that of meditation or dreaming, the intellect is now open to all possibilities. A *Tsalah* (rib) is taken. Tsalah is 90.30.70.5—all feminine numbers, meaning fertile possibilities, the opposite of rigid certainty. 90 is the quintessential feminine directional energy, which uses metabolism (30) to build structures, in this case of perception. 70 and 5 tell us what that perception is about: all possibilities (70) that are alive (5) within us—insight, intuition, foresight, and transcendence, activated through intentionality.

And the rib, which the Lord God had
taken from man, made he a woman,
and brought her unto the man.

And the man said, This is now bone of
my bones and flesh of my flesh: she
shall be called Woman, because she
was taken out of Man.

> *Therefore shall a man leave his*
> *father and mother, and shall cleave*
> *unto his wife: and they shall*
> *be as one flesh.*

GENESIS 2:22–24

An interesting point to realize here is the specificity of bones, which represent a unique element in myth. Bones convey essence, that which cannot be eroded away. A Native American myth tells of a princess who restores her father, the chief, to life after a buffalo god has trampled him to death. After gathering up a few scraps of his bones that she finds scattered about, she covers herself with a blanket and begins singing and chanting to them. The bones soon grow flesh and assume the form of her beloved father. This is, essentially, an act of resurrection. The bones, because they contain essence, have the ability to resurrect life.

There are a few sacred myths in Mexico and Central and South America about an old crone who finds the bones of animals in the desert. She beats the bones together while chanting the song of life and the bones grow flesh, becoming living creatures again.

My favorite of these bones-to-life stories is "Skeleton Woman," retold by Clarissa Pinkola Estes in her marvelous book *Women Who Run With the Wolves: Myths and Stories of the Wild Woman Archetype* (New York: Ballantine Books, 1992). The wild woman archetype, by the way, is a clear representation of the energies and potentials in the frontal lobes. "Skeleton Woman" illustrates the importance of bone imagery in myth.

A young woman, for a forgotten reason, was tossed into the sea. Many years later a fisherman hooked her skeleton on his line. When he saw what he'd reeled in, he fearfully ran back to his hut, but Skeleton Woman, caught fast to his line, clinked and clanked noisily behind him. As he rushed through the door of his hut, she tumbled into a pile at his feet. Looking at her then, he took pity upon her fate and straightened out all her bones so that at least she resembled what she formerly had been. This being a difficult task, he then fell deeply asleep. Skeleton Woman saw a tear squeeze out of his eye and realized she was thirsty. She drank and drank and drank from his tear. The water gave her strength. She then cut open the man's chest, took out his heart, and began chanting and singing with its beating rhythm. As she sang, her flesh grew back until she was a complete woman again. She then placed the man's heart back in his chest, healed the wound, sang his clothes off, and climbed into bed with him.

As a mythological image, bones represent essence, a solidity (like that in stones, equated with the solidity of truth) that cannot be destroyed and from which life resurrects itself in ever more complex models. In Genesis, the woman is crafted from one of Adam's bones— and not just any bone, but a rib bone, that which protects the heart, the region of love and purity.

In the human brain's evolution the frontal lobes arose from the neocortex, which had previously evolved from a division of the limbic system specializing in vision. This is evolution's pattern. It moves in the direction of more complexity, arising out of material already present. Eve was crafted from one of Adam's ribs, just as the frontal lobes emerged from a portion of the neocortex. She emerged as a more advanced, compassionate, loving, intuitive, and insightful neural substrate. She is the heart within the mind because she was crafted from a symbolic rib bone, the protector of the heart's intentions.

The prefrontal cortex offers the most advanced neural potentials in the human brain. But there is no cultural and academic framework on which to mold that potential. Science, playing the part of the diabolical stepmother, sometimes seems bent on invalidating her attributes— intuition and other extrasensory abilities—often refusing to acknowledge their presence, much less their contribution to human neural functioning. The vast majority of us have experienced transcendent events, spiritual visions, miraculous healings, near-death experiences, and the like, and a number of cultures have incorporated such things into their way of life. For example, the Australian Aborigines, for thousands of years, have used intuition and telepathy as powerful survival and communication skills; their cultural values recognize the worth of such tools. Because science cannot explain such "phenomena," however, it has often denied the validity of such experiences.

Logical reasoning, when confronted with the unknown and its vast possibilities, often uses denial to explain away what it can't fit within familiar paradigms of certainty. This is how continuity functions in the brain, limiting and restricting our thought and imagination. As a result, the attributes of the frontal lobes are often devalued, dismissed, trivialized, and outright denied by the very cortex in the brain that names and defines. The prefrontal cortex is denied her authentic identity, as Eve is certainly denied hers by Western religious authorities interpreting this myth.

The rest of the Genesis story is orchestrated by this archetypal woman, who, by the way, is still nameless. Adam has not yet defined her enough to give her an authentic name. He merely recognizes that she exists, specifically as *opposite* to himself. So he names them both, defining their differences as opposites, which is all he is capable of perceiving at this time.

> . . . *she shall be called Woman,*
> *because she was taken out of Man.*
>
> GENESIS 2:23

The Hebrew word for *woman,* Esha, means "inner fire" or "inner flame." Esha is a wonderful representation of the transcendental potentials of inspiration, insight, and foresight that are encapsulated within the frontal lobes. Each of those potentials refers to light, now internalized within the human brain in a story that began with the creation of light on the first day.

The man and woman here are essentially new beings. The man is not Adam, but Eesh (Man), and the woman is Esha (Woman). They have both been transformed from the generic "male and female" first introduced in Genesis 1:27. The fact that they are now named Eesh and Esha, "Man" and "Woman," means that they have achieved a fertile state, just as the words *man* and *woman* designate such a state in modern biological terms. This is not a fertility of the body, however, but a fertility of the mind, psyche, and spirit, represented by the transcendental qualities of neural fire, such as intuition and intentionality. Eesh and Esha represent the final element: Fire. Earth, Air, and Water appeared in Genesis 1. With Eesh and Esha we now have the inner fire of intentionality that births transcendental awareness.

The next verse reveals a very important message, if you know about the brain and its four cortexes. It reveals Adam's next, and most important, directive in terms of reorienting the intellect and organizing balance and wholeness in the brain and psyche.

THE FOURTH DIRECTIVE

Therefore shall a man leave his
father and his mother and shall
cleave unto his wife . . .

GENESIS 2:24

Quite plainly, the verse states that "a man . . . shall *cleave* unto his wife," not the other way around, as patriarchal culture insists. *He* should leave his evolutionary family—the neural heritage of sensory continuity in the r-complex and limbic system—and go to *her,* forming a bond with her transcendent potentials. She remains where she is, steadfast and pure, while he moves away from evolutionary continuity toward a new union with revolutionary new neural potential and possibilities. She is the unknown of extrasensory potentials within himself, the most powerful being the nonsensory gift of intentionality.

This is a profound statement, the culmination of the preceding acts. He must first find her, then name her, then finally cleave unto her. The neocortex must leave his own father and mother—the r-complex and limbic system, source of the patterns of continuity in the brain—and instead cleave unto the unknown, disruptive, feminine fire of the frontal lobes, which will initiate a new transcendent pattern for the mind and psyche, and for human society.

In this new pattern, the intellectual energy of the neocortex is not diminished in any way because it has already been fully developed by Western academics. It does not lose its independence when it makes this move. On the contrary, it takes along that independence and marries it to the fragile potentials of the frontal lobes. This initiates an enormous release of new fertility and fecundity in the brain. In such a union, the fully developed intellectual support of the neocortex is put at the prefrontal cortex's disposal, nurturing and protecting her so she can unfold her sparkling transcendent nature.

By cleaving unto Esha, Eesh leaves behind the old evolutionary identity of survival of the fittest and all that goes with it. The agenda of continuity and certainty in the brain uses dominance, aggression, and predation as major strategies because they fostered the survival of the genes that created the first three cortexes. That is evolution's way and it has been the intellect's way. But no longer is it to be the way for Adam, who is being called upon in these verses to abandon it and move forward into the unknown, to intentionality and transcendence. If Adam is to remain true to his new identity as Eesh, by cleaving unto Esha, the inner fire of the frontal lobes, he must abandon the old dog-eat-dog world of Newtonian certainties in the survival-oriented intellect. For him that intellect is now regressive. This is how he *betrays* the bad master he has been and learns, instead, to be a good servant to new, fertile possibilities in awareness.

By cleaving unto Esha he recognizes, respects, and appreciates her agenda, which is transcendence and integration, and begins to function out of authentic masculinity by protecting her territory. Hers is a new directive for life and the only way to fully develop human potential.

And they were both naked, the man
and his wife, and were not ashamed.

GENESIS 2:25

The truth that is now naked in the naming of Esha and Eesh, that they both now recognize, is the renewing, rejuvenating, and often playful function of disruptive possibilities embodied in the firelike energy of the frontal lobes. Prefrontal energy disrupts rigid thought and old intellectual patterns in the neocortex, burning obsolete behaviors and paradigms to ashes in the flames of innovation. This power also ignites the intellect.

Disruption is the unknown penetrating the known, timelessness penetrating time, intention penetrating evolution. It is transcendence. Adam's new role is to make this space sacred, to determine its boundaries and be a vigilant protector of them by ensuring that they remain "naked," or, as in "the naked truth," revealed.

EESH AND ESHA

The enormous struggle to bring about this recognition has finally been fruitful. But this tale is far from over. Now, together, Eesh and Esha must battle the old remnants of rigidity, continuity, and certainty in the brain (and in Western culture) in order to free, develop, shape, and form their *intention* for integration into a *reality* of wholeness.

Eesh and Esha's new partnership offers a new model for humanity. It integrates the opposites of masculine and feminine, as Adam begins to understand the protective role of authentic masculinity, specifically designed to safeguard his opposing intelligence contained in the feminine frontal lobes.

In order to achieve neural integration from a state of patriarchal consciousness, it is necessary for the masculine neocortex to humble himself and reach for the feminine prefrontal cortex. She is the central pillar around which he wraps himself, like ivy stretching toward the light. He must cease his narcissistic behavior and attitudes and become knightly, protecting and admiring the qualities of the feminine.

Eesh and Esha represent the two most advanced forms of intelligence and potential in the brain. The neocortex and frontal lobes are two opposites, one prompted by time and the other by timelessness, one by rationale and the other by transcendent intentions. As these two integrate, the interplay between time and timelessness becomes active, which actualizes more fertility and fecundity in awareness and results in more creativity in daily life.

The fact that the Qabalists depicted Adam as the one to change perspective (as a result of completing the four directives) signals the critical act of recognition. Adam's change in intellectual perspective to that of Eesh, due to his recognition of Esha's powers, determines the relationship between the two as a new pattern, one in which the revolutionary new potentials in the frontal lobes are not dismissed, devalued, and abandoned—as they have been, among us, by patriarchal attitudes—but instead are recognized, admired, and respected because Adam has a new vision of his opposite, with whom he is now aligned.

This new vision inspires a new attitude that allows the fiery potentials of the frontal lobes to ignite and also allows a new potential to flame up within the neocortex. Such a mutually beneficial relationship, the result of an interplay between opposites, is the foundation of transcendence, promoting a continual interplay between certainties and possibilities. The result of such an interplay would fulfill a statement made by British mathematician Alfred North Whitehead, "The art of progress is to preserve order amid change—and to preserve change amid order."

The way in which this new partnership is activated in the psyche is one of the deepest mysteries the Qabalists understood. What it does, essentially, is provide a pattern of continual personal growth through a new dynamic of awareness. That new dynamic is based on the interplay between the outer world (which the neocortex sees) and the inner world (which the frontal lobes see). The outer world of the self is its behavior. The inner world of the self is its awareness and intentionality. As behavior and intention interact, they each change the other, subtly and continually, which results in the development of grace and wisdom, and more grace and more wisdom, ad infinitum. Is this not an angelic state? This is the pattern and journey of personal growth activated through the interplay of opposites in the psyche, now on fire with new awareness.

One other thing needs to be mentioned concerning neural integration. When the neocortex and frontal lobes integrate themselves into transcendent functioning, they then also lift the two oldest cortexes—the r-complex and limbic system—into higher functioning with them. It doesn't happen all at once, but is an ongoing process. The entire brain eventually becomes rewired and reorganized for higher purposes—for quality of life, for meaning, joy, and happiness, for creativity—not just for survival.

But we are merely at the beginning of this new dynamic in Genesis. In the next chapter, which reinterprets Genesis 3, Esha takes the initiative in the integrative process now that Adam is cleaving unto her, because he finally recognizes her special powers, the unique visual mechanisms of the frontal lobes: insight, foresight, and intention.

5

Descent into the Psyche
and the Struggle of Opposites

So far in the Genesis story the two worlds have been defined, the cosmological *outer* world of evolution in Genesis 1 and the mythological *inner* world of the brain and psyche in Genesis 2. With Genesis 3 the story now descends deep into the psyche's microcosm, illuminating its activities.

The mythology presented in Genesis reveals life's interplay of opposites. That interplay fertilizes growth. In this case, it is growth in personal awareness because this story is taking place deep in the recesses of human neural tissue.

The psyche's goal, in this respect, is to grow and self-generate wholeness, characterized by psychological clarity, which in turn produces happiness and creativity for solving problems. Such a state cannot be attained, however, without a struggle. That struggle is between two opposing forces—continuity and disruption (or certainties and possibilities)—active everywhere in the cosmos, and definitely in the psyche. This struggle is epitomized in our personal lives when we learn the difference between merely existing and living authentically. This is what we wrestle with as we attempt to balance our needs for survival with the needs of the soul.

Survival is important, as we all know, but so is soul. During the textile workers strike in Lawrence, Massachusetts, in 1912, the strikers adopted as one of their slogans "Bread and Roses," with bread symbolizing the need for survival and roses symbolizing the needs of the soul. The strikers insisted they needed both. We cannot be whole without expressing both, in balance. That balance is forfeited when survival needs are glamorized by a corporate culture that glorifies them out of all proportion to necessity. As we enter into this new millennium, balance is struggling to be reinstated. According to the Qabalists, the place to begin is within the psyche. Only by starting there do we develop an authentic perspective of balance so that we can then re-create it in the outer world of culture. Genesis 3 is the story of regaining balance. Before we investigate this part of the myth, let's look at the familiar story of David and Goliath, which is told later in the Old Testament and which also represents the pattern of imbalance trying to correct itself.

DAVID AND GOLIATH

The story of David and Goliath depicts the struggle between opposing energies in the psyche, the difference between the frontal lobes and the rest of the brain. The forces of continuity and certainty are represented neurophysiologically, as our survival needs. Having been established through evolution and patriarchal culture, they are immense, like the Philistine giant Goliath. The opposing energies of soul, spirit, and psyche in the frontal lobes—the forces of disruption, innovation, fun, and possibilities—are invested in the image of David (whose descendant was Jesus), the young Israelite man who battled Goliath. Soul attributes must wrestle their way into consciousness and win a place for themselves, because winning, for them, means integration for us. Yet the forces represented by David have no muscle. There hasn't been a long evolutionary or cultural cycle to recognize, develop, and establish any. So David's strength is no match for Goliath's.

At the same time, David symbolizes a radically different kind of energy, fleeting and impermanent. It comes to us in discreet and mysterious dreams, or pops into consciousness unexpectedly in the middle of a busy day, when we often do not think we have time for exploration. Yet all it seeks, initially, is *recognition*. One of the best ways to recognize disruption and possibilities is through playfulness and fun, which balance the serious side of life, like responsibility and survival. The specific symbol of disruptive potential in the David and Goliath story is David's aim, his special skill. He is a sharpshooter, gifted in using a slingshot. Although David is not strong, he uses a different kind of power and brings down the giant Goliath with a small pebble. This is what recognition does. It is a seemingly tiny skill, yet its aim is uncannily accurate and its power is undeniable.

David represents the tiny flame of disruptive intentionality and its unknown possibilities in the frontal lobes battling Goliath, the gigantic tide of continuity and certainty invested in the r-complex, limbic system, and neocortex. Disruption offers our spirit of transcendence a presence. With that presence it knocks on the door of continuity and survival needs in the psyche, requesting to be integrated into the psyche's life in order to keep us in touch with all the possibilities waiting in the wings of our potential.

The story of David and Goliath is a classic tale of the underdog who triumphs against overwhelming odds. Spirit, with its element of timelessness, is the underdog because the forces of continuity and certainty (for survival needs) in the brain are much bigger and stronger, like Goliath. The Goliath aspect of our neural world is an enormous network of neural channels that produce our thoughts, behaviors, and attitudes for survival. David, on the other hand, is etched ever so slightly in our dreams, hopes, and fleeting visions of what we can become in solving the problems that plague us. Each of us participates in the David and Goliath struggle when our brain labors to birth its self-awareness, which is why we identify so much with such stories.

In the Indiana Jones films—another series of stories based on a mythological model replicating actual psychological events—a mild-mannered anthropology professor, a "geek" in today's jargon, embarks on fantastic adventures, battling predatory monsters and humans in order to save the day and discover the magic element. Indiana is a modern David, the small, insignificant man struggling against something much bigger than he. Such tales are allegories of the psyche's journey to wholeness, struggling to integrate previously suppressed, denied, or unrecognized energies. Likewise, artists exemplify the spirit of David. A "starving artist" is one who chooses soul needs over survival needs, attempting to integrate the soul's creative desires into everyday life.

Genesis 3 contains the same theme, reminding us that it is within our ability to expand our own inner vision. This part of the Genesis story tells of a woman who eats a fruit that opens not only her eyes, but Adam's eyes too. If we wish to truly understand this story, we must figure out why she does not die when she eats the fruit that carries the punishment of death. We must figure out how, upon eating that dangerous fruit, she not only cheats death and transforms herself, but somehow also passes these amazing qualities on to Adam so that he won't die either and his eyes will also be opened. This is her role as the helpmate, which has gone unnoticed for three thousand years because the story has not been interpreted by minds that are alive with light.

Esha's Pivotal Conversation

One of the ways in which disruptive energy is portrayed in this section of Genesis is through the fact that Esha does not yet have her real name. Adam has named her merely Esha—"woman." Esha/Woman is generically fertile, as is Eesh/Man. She is not yet Eve, the mother of all living, which is what her intentionality is striving for and what she will eventually achieve when Adam finally recognizes her fully and names her. She does not yet have *that* name because she has not yet developed her fertility into creativity.

The reason for this is that we who are reading the story do not yet understand the meaning and purpose of transcendence. We don't understand that to be spiritually adept is to be in relationship with everything around us, to interact with one another, to be fully engaged in our world. True spirituality is not accomplished merely through meditation, zazen (Zen sitting), ritual, or worship: experiences that isolate us from the world. Authentic spirituality is accomplished only when our meditations yield action, full participation in the world. In this myth it is the woman who takes action after Adam has finally recognized her.

Esha, in Genesis 3, wastes no time in stoking the engines of intention that lead to personal growth, integration, and clarity. She begins by entering into the most dangerous conversation ever recorded—or so we have been led to believe—an exchange with the serpent, which takes place beneath the branches of the tree of the knowledge of good and evil. The result of this conversation was very serious, we have been told: the downfall of the entire human race. If we view it mythologically, however, with Dr. MacLean's information in mind, we may see this conversation with an entirely new perspective, and can appreciate a new image of the archetypal woman.

Esha represents the essence of disruptive energy within the psyche, timelessness. Hers is the inner fire of gestational power, the capacity to develop potentiality into actuality. Potential originates in timelessness, in the unknown. Included in the illusions of the patriarchal perspective are that the unknown is something evil and that learning must be undertaken only with discipline and seriousness. Esha is the container of our transcendence, the womb of our genius, the birthing element of all our as yet unrealized possibilities, including play and fun, which we are finally beginning to recognize as essential elements of learning.

Esha reveals the unknown as potential, *living* potential, because it has the possibility of being actualized if it is recognized. When Adam finally realizes this, he names her, in Genesis 3:20, ". . . Eve, because she was the mother of all *living.*" She transforms from Esha, the fertile state, into perpetual pregnancy, Hhevah, a symbolic mother, representative of all the pregnant possibilities within us that we activate through recognition and intention.

The serpent Esha encounters represents the qualities of the human brain's reptilian cortex (the r-complex), primarily willpower, its major drive. When we are learning any type of new information, the energies we call on the most are motivation and attention. These major components of willpower are released in the r-complex. Not coincidentally, a bundle of nerve fibers called the *locus ceruleus,* originating in the r-complex, builds long, looping pathways of communication throughout the brain, more or less like a hairnet. These pathways are a major influence on any goal we may strive to reach, and certainly influence the psyche's goal of growing its own wholeness through neural integration.

The main neurochemical the fibers of the locus ceruleus release is *noradrenaline,* which has a powerful affect on motivation and attention. Noradrenaline prompts the release of *nerve growth factor,* a substance that encourages the brain to generate and regenerate neural connections, strengthening communicative activities throughout the brain. In one experiment, scientists removed half of a rat's brain, then directed it to walk a plank, which it had been trained to do prior to the surgery. The rat could not perform, naturally, because half its brain was gone. Three hours after it had been injected with noradrenaline, however, the rat successfully completed its task because the boost in intraneural communication prompted by noradrenaline was so strong that it even compensated for the missing half of the rat's brain.

While half of our brains haven't been physically removed, essential parts have been repressed and suppressed as a result of patriarchal perspectives. Willpower, therefore, is a handy tool to use during a hero's journey of integration. It helps us maintain our motivation and focus in the face of the often overwhelming odds of our own doubts, fears, and insecurities, especially those concerning who we are, how we fit into society, and how we engage in personal growth within a culture that often resists it.

Willpower is also a form of desire. When we will ourselves to learn something new—whether it be real estate law or how to integrate a compartmentalized psyche—we are desiring knowledge, power, and control. This desire cum willpower is made possible by the locus ceruleus and the release of noradrenaline originating in the reptilian cortex of the human brain, which supplies our motivation and attention.

The serpent, then, is a fitting mythological representation of scientific fact, the functions of the r-complex with regard to motivation and attention, willpower, and desire. When seen in the light of the possibility of focusing willpower on the goal of attaining wisdom—which is what Esha desires in Genesis—a radical new interpretation of this conversation emerges.

Esha's desire is for inner knowledge and personal growth. It is pure and therefore empowers her inner life. This inner power also focuses the intellect in a new direction, because Adam is now cleaving unto her, perhaps one of the most important spiritual and psychological imperatives we ever learn. When we harness the r-complex's powers to support our desires for internal growth, they become invaluable in our search for happiness and fulfillment—our heaven. In the following verse, the r-complex talks to Esha.

> *For God doth know that in the*
> *day ye eat thereof, then your*
> *eyes shall be opened, and ye shall be as*
> *the gods, knowing good and evil.*
>
> GENESIS 3:5

What a wondrous message! Her eyes will be opened and she will be as the gods, knowing good and evil. What could be a more powerful motivator than that? Who wouldn't want to be as the gods: all powerful, having full control over one's life; and all knowing, having the wisdom to live life fully? Because this is Esha's life—the life of the frontal lobes—it means the actualization of her agenda: integration, clarity, and transcendence, which lead to creative problem solving.

Notice that the serpent never talks to Adam, but only to Esha. She is the only one who receives this message of transcendence, and not from an outer God, but from an inner source.

A TREE TO MAKE ONE WISE

And when Esha *saw that the tree was good for food, and that it was pleasant to the eyes, a tree to be desired to make one wise, She took of the fruit thereof, and did eat, and gave also unto her husband with her; and he did eat.*

GENESIS 3:6

A tree to be desired to make one wise—what could be more noble than that? This is an extraordinary circumstance. Esha is not desiring power, wealth, or status, the so-called worldly goods of survival; instead she desires wisdom and spiritual goods that will lead to wholeness and integration.

This desire makes her strong and courageous because it is pure. Remember, she was crafted from Adam's rib, the bone that protects the heart, the region of love and purity. She is seeking not power to dominate—patriarchy's power—but rather the power to integrate, muscle and strength for soul intentions. Therefore, she is not afraid to question the *perceived* outer authority of a *perceived* outer God. She listens to the serpent, because he is an opposing part of her own neural anatomy. If she eats the fruit of this tree, her eyes will be opened and her desire for wisdom will be fulfilled. To Esha, inner wisdom is worth far more than outer obedience. She does not hesitate.

But how does the serpent know what he does? Why should he be the one to point out that the fruit will open her eyes? And why does he point this out to her and not to Adam?

In neural terms, the serpent represents the r-complex and Esha represents the frontal lobes. They are the "lowest" and "highest" cortexes in the brain, one masculine, the other feminine. During this conversation they are beginning the integration process of uniting the separate cortexes by talking to each other, strengthening the communicative networks between them. This act represents the humble beginnings of the heroic inner accomplishments in this myth, which are to integrate the brain by unifying the separate and unconnected elements within it, modifying and redirecting the agendas of the older cortexes to include spiritual fulfillment in their daily routines of survival. In order to do that, it is essential that they communicate with each other, beginning with the two that are farthest away from each other, evolutionarily speaking: the r-complex and the frontal lobes. In essence, during this conversation, the reptilian drive for survival is being integrated with the frontal lobe desire for transcendence.

A major aspect of neural integration is recognizing that until we accept the heroic challenge and begin the integration process, our psyche remains compartmentalized and isolated from other elements in the brain. In such a state it is confused, scattered, and shortsighted, unable to aid us in living the life we want to live. In these verses Esha is recognizing that the path to wisdom is through intraneural connection and integration, not through obedience to an outer God. If she is to accomplish this heroic task, she must betray God. But because the God of patriarchy is an illusion, she is not actually betraying God. That God doesn't exist. It is only an incomplete mind that imagines a God who demands obedience. So Esha, in eating the fruit, betrays the *illusion* of obedience to an outer God and listens, instead, to the disruptive voice of her own neural potential.

The powers in the frontal lobes, Esha's powers, are the only ones that can take the initiative in the integrative tasks because they are the only neural powers in the brain with the capacity to look inward, peering into the brain itself to see how it is handling the processing of information through symbols. Only by perceiving our inner psychological and neurological activity—such as the neglect of feelings, the alienation of spirit, or the misuse of authority by the neocortex—can the powers of the frontal lobes assess what action to take. Those powers must therefore be activated, by seeking wisdom.

Here, in Genesis, the r-complex is telling Esha, the prefrontal cortex, to take the leadership role in the neural integration process because Adam is now doing his job of cleaving unto her, putting his awesome intellectual powers at her service and protecting her domain. Her first step in that regard is to eat the previously forbidden fruit—the fruit of the tree of the knowledge of good and evil—and to digest it and integrate it with her desire for wisdom.

AND THEIR EYES WERE OPENED

And when Esha saw that the tree was
good for food, and that it was pleasant to
the eyes, a tree to be desired to make one
wise, she took of the fruit thereof and did
eat, and gave also unto her husband
with her, and he did eat.
And the eyes of them both were
opened . . .

GENESIS 3:6–7

Why? What has transformed the fruit so much that instead of killing them, it blesses them by opening their eyes? What did Esha see that was so pleasant?

Just this: She saw the truth that frees us from the prison of continuity. She saw what the Qabalists have presented all along, that the fruit of the famous tree does not contain the knowledge of good and evil. Rather it contains the knowledge of opposites—of continuity and disruption, of time and timelessness, of inner and outer, of mass and energy—which the reader of this text can realize only if it is interpreted according to the Qabalic acronyms that restore the original meanings to the symbols TVB (good) and RA (evil).

In that original meaning, Esha sees that TVB is the "perpetual building of containers" that is often perceived as good (by static minds), while RA is the disruptive energy that bursts through those containers, like a chick hatching from its shell, destroying the shell in the process. The destruction of that obsolete shell has been labeled evil, because we do not see that the destruction of something that has become obsolete is a necessity that simultaneously ignites the birth of new potential.

In order for us to be continually renewed, must we not also continually die to whatever has become obsolete within us? The phoenix rising from the ashes, resplendent in shining new colors, represents the integration of death-in-birth that is generated by a realization of this transcendent nature. In order for the germ to grow, the husk must die. Is this not the way of life? What can be labeled *evil* in that? Why should we not embrace the death as we do the life it allows? If a baby does not "die" to its former life in the womb, it cannot be born to life in the world. If we do not allow obsolete social structures to die, we cannot birth a new culture for ourselves and our shining new spirit to inhabit.

Jesus said we must not put new wine in old bottles. Is this not the same message? This is what Esha realizes when she eats the fruit of that famous tree, the tree of the knowledge of TVB and RA. What she realizes, and this realization is *the* transcendent experience, is that there is no good or evil, not here, not anywhere. Good and evil—like a flat earth—are perceptual illusions. They are interpretations that exist only in the mind of an incomplete intellect, which is the state of all patriarchal intellects.

The awareness of the interplay between continuity and disruption, between matter and energy, between structure and process, is the wisdom and knowledge the psyche seeks to understand in order to perceive wholeness and integrate itself accordingly. Obsolete definitions of reality, such as good and evil, are burned to ashes and transformed by Esha's new fire of insight and integration. Her awareness is the realization that what was previously perceived as good is actually the static element of continuity (TVB), and what was previously perceived as evil is actually the active element of disruption (RA), a rejuvenating, refreshing and life-giving insight from the unknown.

Hallelujah!

The tree of the knowledge of TVB and RA, continuity and disruption, time and timelessness, certainty and possibilities, *is* the tree of life.

Adam was forbidden the fruit of that symbolic tree because he, patriarchal man, had defined the opposites incorrectly and had thereby sacrificed his own clarity, just as, during Galileo's trial, the Church had defined the universe as a pattern in which the sun revolved around Earth, thereby sacrificing its clarity. Such an intellect seeks to control that which can never be controlled—the forces of disruption—by labeling them *evil*. In defining disruption as evil, the mind is forced to cling to static continuity as *good*. This causes the static energy in the psyche to become too strong, rigid, and inflexible, like Goliath. The Qabalists perceived this as psychological death because it kills our appreciation of disruptive elements. Esha—by eating the fruit that dispels the illusory strength of TVB/good—resurrects the true meaning of disruption in RA (Raysh-Ayn—200.70), which, in Ayn, contains the supreme disruptive element, Aleph.

Esha embodies that disruptive element. For her to eat of that tree means life, not death. By eating the fruit first, Esha reclaims the power of death (permanent rigidity) that Adam was sentenced to if he had eaten it when he was alone. This rescuing of the male by the female symbolizes the integration of the inner and outer worlds through the clarity provided by the frontal lobes. When Esha eats the fruit, she recognizes herself and her innate, feminine, disruptive essence. Then she passes that recognition to Adam along with the fruit she offers him. "Here," she says, "take this fruit because it is the knowledge of opposites—of body and soul, of feminine and masculine, of energy and matter, of time and timelessness, who rejoice in one another because they are mutually self-defining. One cannot exist without the other; therefore, they must embrace one another like germ and husk, like yin and yang. Take it and eat it and see this pleasant realization for yourself." So he does, and he finally sees what she does in Genesis 3:7: "The eyes of them both were opened."

This is the moment of initiation for the archetypal couple. They are initiated into the realm of the gods. They now see that the knowledge of continuity and disruption is the exquisite knowledge of life's interplay between opposites. Disruption is the element that brings timelessness to awareness. This timelessness is what touches every artist, every poet, every writer. Once touched by it, they are so moved they must express it. They write it down, sing its song, tell its story, because it opens their heart and mind to the myriad possibilities hidden within.

MOLTEN EPIPHANY

Insight is that connection to timelessness, to Aleph. It is the secret dowry of the prefrontal cortex, bequeathed to Adam, the intellect, after he has cleaved unto her and begins his authentic masculine task of protecting her intentions. When Esha eats the fruit, digesting its meaning and recognizing its truth, only then can it be shared with Adam, who could not eat it alone because his knowledge base was too rigid and too confined, conditioned by the nature of mass alone and ignorant of the quantum nature of energy.

We all have Adam's tendencies to armor ourselves against the disruptive, fire-filled elements of life, its potent germs. The Bible is a revelation only insofar as it includes the paradox of life-in-death, timelessness-in-time, disruption-in-continuity, thereby disrupting every rational certainty we may cling to so as to aid us in attaining a vision of life as a continual becoming and unfolding of possibility and potentiality.

The purpose of these disruptions within the psyche, as surgings of

Aleph/timelessness, is to instigate our psychological, spiritual, and neural growth. The flame of Aleph lights the fire of our becoming, fertilizing new vision that sees how to solve problems and integrate spiritual ideals into everyday life. What Esha realizes when she eats the fruit is that death, in the form of disruption and timelessness, is actually here every moment as a vibrant crescendo in our own psychological symphony.

This is the very epicenter of the myth, its deepest point of descent into the psyche. When we come to realize that we are all continually waging a battle between the agenda of continuity invested in the three older cortexes of our own brain (Goliath) and the intuitive, disruptive fire emanating from the Aleph hidden within the highly sensitive neurology of the frontal lobes (symbolized by David and Esha), we come to realize that the only way we can win the struggle for freedom is to form an alliance with Aleph. By forming such an alliance, we take on the mantle of the disruptive hero who battles the enormous forces of the status quo.

To the Qabalists, this is the quintessential moment. The human mind, especially under the influence of patriarchy, is prone to becoming static. In a static state, it falls under the spell of illusory beliefs. Under the spell of illusory beliefs we may blame our suffering on God or, worse, engage in suicidal acts of monstrous proportions, like those of September 11, because we think that to do so will allow us to live in heaven with seventy virgins. It seems absurd, but the power of illusory beliefs is all too real.

Therefore, what Adam and Esha have just witnessed is crucial. The introduction of disruption into a static mind is what saves it from itself. Disruption, the witnessing of the timeless element of life, kicks the static mind into life again, much as the electric paddles used by doctors revive a heart that has stopped. Disruption shatters a static state and in so doing allows the energies of life to invade awareness.

This is the image of Christ nailed to the cross. Aleph/timelessness is the cross. The body of Christ, bound and nailed to that cross, is an image that depicts the ongoing disruption of the continuity of body existence and survival consciousness by Aleph's timeless, transcendent presence. When we bond ourselves to Aleph/timelessness, it liberates us to the vitality of ever-fresh, latent potential, ushering in a new direction in life, a new framework for culture, a fertilizing of dreams and hopes.

The transcendental juice, the hot, molten epiphany that results from contact with Aleph, is what the three oldest cortexes are so often anxious about. They don't want that contact with the hot flame of the unknown. They want things to stay the way they have been—continuity in existence—because that way *seems* safe, familiar, and comfortable. It is survival. But not Esha. She is free from their fears. She embodies the molten heat because her name means "inner fire." Like lava erupting from within the earth's center, she pours her new, transcendent vision over the landscape of the brain, reshaping its neural maps of perception.

The challenge is for each of us to do the same, awakening to the intensity of latent fire within us, allowing the timelessness of RA to invade our awareness.

FIG LEAVES OF ILLUSION AND REVELATION

And the eyes of them both were
opened, and they knew that they
were naked; and they sewed fig leaves
together, and made themselves aprons.

GENESIS 3:7

According to traditional interpretations, the fact that Adam and Esha are naked means that they are also ashamed, for they begin making fig-leaf aprons with which to cover themselves. This whole shame business is actually one of the illusory beliefs originating from the static rationale of the neocortex. Shame is a domination tactic. For three thousand years religious doctrine has decreed that Adam and Esha are covering themselves because they are naked and ashamed. Yet read the verse. It says nothing about shame. It says "they knew they were naked," but it doesn't say anything about being ashamed of this. The shame is purely illusory. It has never existed except in the static minds of religious authorities who have decreed it.

Shame is a powerful psychological weapon that can be used to diminish and therefore control others, especially when it is associated with nakedness. We "civilized" people have an abhorrence of being naked, believing nakedness reveals our flaws. But in reality, scientific investigation has proved that nakedness has a calming affect on people. It decreases aggression. In other words, being naked makes us more human. By seeing and accepting the physical flaws of others and ourselves as revealed by nakedness, we become more compassionate. Shame is an illusory belief that has been foisted upon us by a religious elite completely out of touch with its own humanity. Generally, it is a patriarchal assumption with only one purpose: to dominate others by making them feel inadequate.

According to religious doctrine, we are all shameful because we are descendants of this first man and woman. Yet Adam and Esha were never historical people. That's another illusion. They are archetypes in the psyche. As archetypes, they made aprons, yes, but not because they were ashamed. Aprons have a specific purpose and it is protection.

When my mother put on an apron (when she used to cook), it was to protect her clothes from spills and grease. When workmen, such as welders, use aprons, they do so to protect themselves and their clothes from sparks or other workplace dangers. Aprons, far from being associated with shame, are worn to protect. If that is so, you might be asking, what are Adam and Esha protecting?

To give you a little insight into Qabalic interpretation, "sewing together" is *Taphar*, Tav-Phay-Raysh, 400.80.200. This indicates the universal resistance to destruction (400) coupled with all undifferentiated individual potential (80), encapsulated within a cosmic pattern (200). It refers to the new awareness—the potential joy—that intellect and intuition have perceived in each other, their opposites. This new potential for joy offers its own resistance (to destruction) for all the new, unstructured potential yet to be realized within the brain. The sewing together is the weaving of this new awareness into the very fibers of consciousness.

They have just had their eyes opened to the transcendent nature of timelessness/disruption. What they need to do, at this point, is protect this precious insight, which is precisely what they do, metaphorically, by sewing together fig leaves. Fig leaves—what could be a more potent symbol for the new possibilities that disruption/Aleph ushers in than a fruit with hundreds of tiny seeds tucked inside of it? It is a marvelous image of fertility and fecundity.

This revelation is their armor and protection against the forces of continuity in the brain that seek to engulf them in survival and domination consciousness. David had his pebbles, his aim, his recognition, which he used in his struggle with Goliath. Adam and Esha have their protective aprons of fig leaves, their recognition of the possibilities of what transcendence can mean for human consciousness and human culture. This protection allows them to grow in awareness, to transcend survival needs and domination tactics in order to fulfill the soul and free the spirit.

The agenda of domination in the brain has become entrenched through patriarchal social conditioning. Adam and Esha's precious new insight of life must do battle with that conditioning in order to keep itself alive. Protected with their aprons of truth, they are going to battle this rigid, dominating, repressive mentality that, through its patriarchal values, has conditioned our awareness. Repressive energies diminish and trivialize the role of tenderness and affection in human relationships and the need to risk contact with the unknown for the sake of psychological renewal.

COSMIC VOCATION

And they heard the voice of the
Lord God walking in the garden
in the cool of the day: and Adam
and his wife hid themselves from the
presence of the Lord God amongst
the trees of the garden.

GENESIS 3:8

This is one of those perplexing narratives that translators usually consider merely poetic. How does a voice *walk* and why is it so important to mention how *cool* the weather is? If we decode it, an altogether new picture emerges.

The Hebrew for *voice* is Qowl, (Qof-Waw-Lammed), 100.6.30. Qof is Aleph-in-duration (100) integrating with or fertilizing (6) organic metabolism (30). Its literal meaning comes from a root word that means "to call aloud, to proclaim, to announce." *Walking* is Halak, Hay-Lammed-final/Khaf, 5.30.500. This translates as universal life (5) in organic metabolism (30) engendering a cosmic pattern of life (500). In one sense this acronym means "to carry" as a "tale bearer." The word *cool* is Raysh-Waw-Hay, 200.6.5, and means the encapsulating into a cosmic pattern (200) of a fertilizing agent (6) and the principle of life (5). Its literal meaning is "to blow, as in a breath, an exhalation."

Add it all up and it becomes this: The masculine and feminine essences, intellect and intuition, heard a "calling" to honor the "proclamation" of the impulse of life in the cosmos and in their own being. This is the calling of the cosmic hero, to awaken to fullness. It is what we are all called to in becoming autonomous, free of nature's repetitive instinctuality and culture's conditioning, in shedding those old skins and being reborn through the cosmic song that sings within.

The rest of the verse seems completely misleading: "And Adam and

Esha hid themselves from the presence of the Lord God amongst the trees of the garden." But again, a hidden picture emerges through Qabalah.

The word *hid* is Chaba, Hay–Bayt–Aleph, 5.2.1. It is associated with another word that means "to cherish, to hide in one's bosom," as in keeping close to one's heart. The acronym is three archetypes: life (5), structure (2), and germ (1). Adam and Esha are not hiding because they are guilty and deceptive, as ecclesiastical translations imply. They are hiding their new awareness the way a germ is tucked inside its husk, a secret dowry awaiting its time of ripening. They are protecting it from the forces of continuity in existence and domination that wish to engulf and absorb it. By doing this, they are following the pattern of life, tucking this new awareness into their bosom, holding it dear, cherishing it, *planting* it among the neural trees in the garden of consciousness. This is a beautiful passage. Its significance is lost, however, in the linguistic version.

But at this time, the dynamics in the psyche have changed. The woman has challenged the commandment, eaten the fruit, gained her wisdom, and passed on to her husband both the fruit and the wisdom. Moreover, neither of them has died, as the commandment said they would. Instead, their eyes have been opened and now they are as the gods, knowing the wisdom of the interplay between opposites that leads to integration and defines wholeness. In other words, the gods, even the Lord God who is now questioning them, no longer have any authority over them.

Adam and Esha now have the same authority as the gods. Remember, the name of the deity changes three times in the course of Genesis, signifying three very different processes. The first name, ELHYM, is a general term for the developing of prototypes that signify organic evolution. YHWH ELHYM is a process that amalgamates the tissue that evolved into the human brain with the awareness that takes place within it. YHWH ELHYM is who we are dealing with here in Genesis 3. This is not an omniscient diety. *It is our own awareness* of whatever we think God is. But it is also a state conditioned by patriarchal consciousness because patriarchy introduced us to literacy, the lens through which we read this story. And this is still *that* seventh day.

The third name of the Lord, YHWH, does not appear until Genesis 4. It represents the final freedom: enlightened perception and transcendent living. Its symbols mean, literally, "existence-life, copulation-life," in which one *H* expresses the life of the container of matter, the body (or husk), and the other *H* is the life of the contained potential, inner fire that is spirit (or germ). These two essential parts of ourselves, in a mature state, are meant to fertilize each other continually, which results in continual personal growth leading to illumination and illumined living. This double impregnation of life, or interplay between opposites, can occur only in human beings. As long as it fails to occur, YHWH is immanent but unrealized. Spirit is present in the flesh, but is inactive.

Our cosmic vocation, according to the story of Genesis, is to actively birth this spirit of interplaying opposites, this potential— YHWH—within ourselves, within the brain that ELHYM has produced, freeing YHWH to act alone—that is, without the baggage of patriarchal (or any cultural) perspective. When YHWH has been achieved, it will produce a new cycle of creation on this planet, our possible future as an integrated humanity.

YHWH ELHYM, the Lord God, the name of the deity in Genesis 3, is merely a reflection of Adam and Esha's psychological state. It is the awareness that our consciousness is trapped in patriarchal perspective and that there is only one way out, through Esha's imperative.

A new insight in the brain is like a seed. It needs to be buried in the rich nutrients of our neural ground (Adamah) so that it can germinate and grow strong enough to generate new roots and branches. Because this ground is the brain, the new roots and branches are parts of a neural system. The new neural system that begins growing involves the precious insights pertaining to wholeness, specifically the role of disruptive transcendence as it battles the brain's forces of continuity and domination. Adam and Esha are not hiding from the Lord God in fear;

they are hiding their new insight in much the same way we plant a seed, so it can do what it is designed to do. Hiding it, in this sense, not only protects it, but allows the possibility of germination as well.

PROCLAIMING VICTORY

And the Lord God called unto Adam,
and said unto him, Where art thou?
And he said, I heard thy voice in
the garden, and I was afraid, because
I was naked; and I hid myself.

GENESIS 3:9–10

When Adam voices his doubts, they aren't doubts about the Lord God alone. They are also doubts about his new (naked) realization, because he understands its vulnerability within a psyche that is rigid from too much patriarchy, domination, and repression. He has taken on the role of protecting the feminine, the revelations of wholeness ushered in through insight, while they develop and grow strong, like Darwin secretly writing his book for twenty-five years, knowing that the world of his time would resist it ferociously. So he waits, and hides, in order to protect and cherish.

And he said, Who told thee that
thou wast naked? Hast thou eaten
of the tree, whereof I commanded
thee that thou shouldst not eat?

And the man said, The woman whom
thou gavest to be with me, she gave
me of the tree and I did eat.

And the Lord God said unto the
woman, What is this that thou
hast done? And the woman said,
The serpent beguiled me, and I
did eat.

GENESIS 3:11–13

YHWH ELHYM is the voice of patriarchal authority attempting to call Adam and Esha back to obedience, back to shame, back to domination and repression through fear. Things have changed, however. This once powerful voice no longer has the same authority over them that it once had. They are now equal to the gods. Trouble is, equality takes some getting used to. In a mind habituated to obeying fearful authorities, it isn't easy to assert one's autonomy. Adam and Esha struggle with this. They are asked questions about obedience and it appears as though they are assessing blame in their answers, but is that what is actually occurring?

Read the verses again. Could Adam, instead of blaming Esha, actually be proclaiming her as the one who brought him to his new transcendent realization? The word *afraid,* when translated, is more like *revered.* Could he not be proclaiming the powers of intuition, insight, and foresight, the powers of the frontal lobes, as stronger than any outer authority in revealing life's sweetness, and therefore more trustworthy? Aren't they both proclaiming their victory over continuity—the continuity of fear, shame, and domination, the continuity of obedience to an outer authority who decreed they would die if they ate the fruit? Adam states emphatically, "I did eat." And Esha says exactly the same thing, "I did eat." Could they not be proclaiming a victory? We did this thing. We ate the fruit, but we didn't die. And not only are we alive, but we now also have our eyes open and are as wise as you.

"The serpent beguiled me" *(Hanahhash hashayiny),* Esha says, and this has been interpreted to mean that she is blaming the serpent for tempting her. Yet *beguiled,* even in English, has two meanings: "seduced" or "tempted"; and "enchanted" or "captivated." What actually happens is this: The serpent *sheens* her. *Sheen* (300)—from *hanahhash hashayiny*—has often been referred to as "cosmic breath," and breathing is a twofold process, consisting of inhaling and exhaling. To *inhale* is to inspire. To *exhale* is to expire. *Expire* has come to mean "death of the body," while to *inspire* is to bring life to the mind. Is this not the cosmic breath of Sheen?

This new perspective changes everything. Instead of blaming each other—an interpretation typical of patriarchal minds—might they be rejoicing in mutual enlightenment and also recognizing who initiated this wonderful circumstance? Adam may be expressing a sentiment more akin to "*She* gave the fruit to me, bless her heart." And likewise, Esha's sentiment may be, "The serpent enchanted me, and I did eat, and am I ever glad I did." Through recognition, this archetypal couple are building bonds of trust between each other.

Remember, YHWH ELHYM is nothing more than a state of awareness we each pass through on our journey to clarity. It is a state we must outgrow in order to allow our inner light to shine forth undiluted. We must accept our divinity, authority, and autonomy, not so we can dominate others or parts of ourselves, but so we can integrate our separate psychological elements and cortexes and discover the trust that wholeness brings.

Notice how the three cortexes—Esha representing the frontal lobes, Adam representing the neocortex, and the serpent representing the r-complex—are all tied up in this activity. There seems to be only one cortex absent, the limbic system. And yet the feelings of joy, identifying with our authentic nature, and memories of trust, which the limbic system directs through its chemistry, are integrating at this very moment in the story. Adam and Esha are valiantly attempting to integrate all those limbic system functions in the face of tremendous fear and the shame, denial, guilt, and oppression with which the Lord God of patriarchy wants to dominate them. Is this not a battle in which we all must engage if we want trust and joy to be part of our lives? Trust is never available through obedience to an outer authority; outer authorities do not have our best wishes in mind, only their own. Obedience to an outer authority is the betrayal of self-trust.

Having said that, I realize certain circumstances involving great danger sometimes necessitate obedience so that a threat can be answered with precision. But most of our daily activities do not involve danger; therefore, obedience is not the daily necessity that patriarchy insists it is.

In these verses Adam and Esha, though perceived as receiving punishment or reprimand, are actually retaining their new revelation. Recognizing the value of disruptive play and fun and allowing feelings, especially those of joy, to express themselves in the face of culture's often overwhelming insistence that life be boring, disciplined, and serious is a remarkable occurrence. So though it appears that the Lord God is dominating them with questions meant to shame, they refuse to be crushed by such declarations. That's the message here. No matter what sort of oppressive energy is hurled at them, it is deflected through their newly acquired vision of the value of disruption and the role that timelessness plays in everyday life: play, fun, joy, insight, intuition, and foresight, essential ingredients of wholeness.

The psyche longs to be whole and healthy. Patriarchy, on the other hand, formed through illusions of incompleteness, seeks to promote its fragmented continuity via obedience patterns, which this newly enlightened couple now reject.

CURSES AND SORROWS

And the Lord God said unto the
serpent, Because thou hast done
this, thou art cursed above all
cattle, and above every beast of
the field; upon thy belly shalt
thou go, and dust shalt thou eat all
the days of thy life:

And I will put enmity between thee
and the woman, and between thy
seed and her seed; it shall bruise
thy head, and thou shalt bruise
his heel.

GENESIS 3:14–15

The original message of these verses turns on the Qabalic definition of the word *cursed*. The acronym translated as *cursed*, ARR, indicates the supreme disruptive force (Aleph) trapped in a double
impenetrable ring of continuity (Raysh-Raysh). This positions the spark
of life within a double husk of resistance from which it is completely
unable to escape. It is a situation that is indeed curselike for the disruptive element itself, trapped in the condition of perpetual continuity. But
this isn't a curse directed toward the serpent because of any wrongdo-
ing. Instead, it is a description of the r-complex's state of development.
Though it is the source of willpower in the human brain, it is nevertheless limited by its own rigidity. As Dr. MacLean noted, it cannot
learn anything new and therefore is instinctively afraid of the unknown,
including all unknown potential.

The r-complex induces us, because of this rigidity, to perform rituals and routines in the face of uneasy situations, such as contacting the
unknown, as a way, however false, of making us feel safe. It strains to
reinforce continuity and familiarity, which, for patriarchy, translates as
punishment, obedience, seriousness, and discipline. "As anyone knows
who has suggested a change in curriculum," MacLean states, "there is
hardly anything more sure to upset emotional and rational minds than
the alteration of long established routines."

The modus operandi of the r-complex seems to be: "Why not simply remain the same, safe in a state of static continuity forever, so that
the unknown need never be considered?" This is the built-in "curse" in
the brain. It sets up a powerful task for the hero, to face the challenge
of the unknown, where disruption and timelessness reside, rather than

turning away from it and remaining insulated in continuity. This is what the verse means when it says, "I will put enmity between thee and the woman, and between thy seed and her seed. . . ." We either challenge the unknown within us or we are cursed by our refusal to do so, because that is our potential and if we refuse to live up to it, we can never claim our authenticity.

> *Unto the woman he said, I will greatly*
> *multiply thy sorrow and thy conception;*
> *in sorrow thou shalt bring forth children;*
> *and thy desire shall be for thy husband,*
> *and he shall rule over thee.*
>
> GENESIS 3:16

This is a sad warning for Esha, stating that her task is a sorrowful one because of the brain's, and patriarchal culture's, rigidity in clinging to the continuity of the known. In sorrow shall she, Esha, bring forth her conception from the unknown, through intuition, insight, and foresight, recognizing the healthy necessity of the timeless aspects of life: play, fun, and feelings. The Sanskrit word *bodhisattva* embodies this same realization—that we must participate in the sorrows of the world, the sorrows of time, so that we can integrate the awareness of timelessness into those sorrows and redeem joy. In this loving participation with the "sorrows of time," latent potential blooms, enabling us to change the neural maps in the brain, to rewire and transform it for joy.

> *And unto Adam he said, Because thou*
> *hast hearkened unto the voice of thy*
> *wife, and hast eaten of the tree, of*
> *which I commanded thee, saying*
> *Thou shalt not eat of it: cursed is the*
> *ground for thy sake; in sorrow shalt*
> *thou eat of it all the days of thy life . . .*
>
> GENESIS 3:17

Notice that it isn't Adam who is cursed, but Adamah (ground). The number equivalent of the Hebrew word for *sorrow* in these verses is 70.90.2–70.90.2.6.700. It means to "carve, fabricate, and hence to worry and fret." We can see here a relationship to consciousness that is only too clear to those who have birthed their own becoming through the "dark night of the soul," carving out for themselves a new awareness of indeterminate possibilities (700).

Whenever we attempt to open our eyes and see clearly the contents of our own being, we are setting a task before ourselves that is incredibly difficult. We are carving from the substance of ourselves the way an artist sculpts a figure out of stone, a new perception of who we are and what we're capable of doing. Considering what culture has taught us, it is a task over which we spend endless hours fretting and worrying, the way a mother worries over her children. The reason the task is so difficult is because we have no model from which to work. All we have is our own potential and our own intent.

> *Thorns also and thistles shall it*
> *bring forth to thee; and thou shalt*
> *eat the herb of the field . . .*
>
> GENESIS 3:18

This is Adam's toil: the prickly thoughts the intellect entertains, the anxieties, inertia, and endless obsessing over things and situations. These are the "herbs of the field" that were present before Adam was created, at the beginning of Genesis 2, that he will now have to eat because he is the one cultivating them. These are his own thoughts and conceptualizations. What better way for the intellect to grow than to have to digest its own thoughts? The deeper realization here is the intellect's processes of growth and purification.

> *In the sweat of thy face shalt thou*
> *eat bread, till thou return unto the*

> *ground; for out of it wast thou taken:*
> *for dust thou art, and unto dust shalt*
> *thou return.*
>
> GENESIS 3:19

Until Adam returns to the state of dust, to the moldable clay of the brain's neural networks of potential, he will never find his true indeterminate image. Through the sweat of his labors he will discover that image, the one that is forever becoming, as a primordial germ, ruled by the feminine gestative power of living fire.

THE MOTHER OF ALL LIVING

> *And Adam called his wife's name*
> *Eve; because she was the mother*
> *of all living.*
>
> GENESIS 3:20

Finally—not until *after* all those curses, sorrows, and reminders are stated—does Esha receive her new name, Eve, or Hhevah, which is Qabalically spelled HWH. It is an obvious preconfiguration for YHWH (Lord), which can be realized only if we study the words of the text from the Qabalic perspective. Adam has finally recognized her essence, so he can finally name her. He couldn't recognize or define that essence until he prevailed through the domination attempt from YHWH ELHYM, which built up his resolve. It heightened his awareness the way Annie Sullivan heightened Helen Keller's when she spelled w-a-t-e-r into Helen's hand as the water gushed through the child's fingers. Finally, through the sheer emotional impact of events, Adam understands who Esha is—the mother of all living, his own authentic human essence as a container of infinite possibilities. He has made the break from evolutionary identity. His essence isn't in what he has been, it isn't in the continuity of the past; it is in what he can become through disruption's invitation, as he seeks to examine every concept and ideology in his mind.

These verses reveal the difficult process of battling the brain's resistance and rigidity, the sorrow and pain that continuity engenders in the brain. By transforming, transfiguring, and integrating the brain's agendas of continuity with the power of disruption/timelessness, we can arrive at a clear perception of life's processes of becoming. Yes, it will be in sorrow. Yes, it will be by the sweat of the brow. Yes, it will constantly demand our attention and toil and pain. It is an image of living energy in the brain, gestating, laboring, and birthing a new vision of autonomy and clarity in the face of the enormity of continuity, patriarchy, and domination.

To fully live we must wrest and wrench and pull and twist and otherwise struggle to extricate our shining, elusive potential from the entrapment of continuity in the brain, because this story takes place in the deepest reaches of the human psyche, not in some external location. We must become David and bring down Goliath. We must be Esha and eat that fruit. We must prevail through the storm of denial that obscures Hhevah, the inner flame of timelessness, shining among the older cortexes who constantly seek to extinguish her light because she upsets their rigid continuity.

The sacred archetypes in this story personify the cosmic interplay of energy and mass, both in the psyche and in the exterior world. They factually are the framework upon which the psyche builds its wholeness. As archetypes, Adam and Hhevah are in us prior even to our birth. Hhevah (Eve) is our living germ of essence, the gestational energy of love, nurturing, wonder, and delight, of joy, trust, and inspiration.

In the movie *Jerry McGuire,* Tom Cruise plays a sports agent who loses his job because he becomes too idealistic. In his attempts to live up to his idealism, he suffers the realization that he alone must shape himself into what he wants to become. This is the suffering of the frontal lobes. They must labor to produce their own image because there are no models to copy. Each of us must build an authentic human identity from the inside out, by living up to our own intentions. There is no model for what an authentic human being is. Each of us alone must create that model. How do we create a model that includes the potentials and possibilities inherent in our indeterminate neural nature? Genesis tells us that we do so by recognizing and integrating Hhevah, our inner flame of disruptive energy.

The purpose of integration is to develop inner authority and autonomy, to "know one's self," and to have that knowledge control our behavior in ways that generate not only the skills that allow us to survive, but also inner happiness and fulfillment so we can thrive. The process of neural integration is one in which the brain learns about itself, and consequently we learn about our deepest fears, doubts, and illusions exposed during this process. We also learn about the powers and forces of rejuvenation as we integrate formerly repressed and suppressed parts of the psyche, especially the feminine energies of feelings and spiritual insight and the childlike qualities of playfulness, fun, and joy.

The curses issued by the Lord God in these verses represent the crumbling of the forces of continuity, external authority, and domination in the psyche as Eve's powers of disruption are finally becoming strong enough to burst through the resistance that has contained them for so long. Adam and Eve are achieving a state of inner psychological and spiritual autonomy by being willing to follow the disruptive insights—the inner fire—of the prefrontal cortex and her intent of integration. Her disruptive energy has finally been recognized as that which gives birth to all potential within us, which becomes new awareness for new behavior. This is our model for authentic humanity. It is a model of becoming because that is our essence. We are new creatures. We can be our own creator. We can create a world based on wholeness, but we must first create that wholeness within ourselves.

The self-generative function of the frontal lobes emerges from the element of disruption and possibilities, not from continuity and certainty. Disruption is living energy because it ushers in new life from the void of the unknown. It is fresh and vital. It is the primordial juice of the universe. This is what Eve's name means. She is the mother of all living essence, representing the germ of our future development, all the indeterminate possibilities that yet await our recognition. She is the wet clay of human potential, waiting to be molded and shaped into her true, indeterminate image.

Eve's association is with possibilities. The recognition of those indeterminate possibilities is our model for being authentically human. Such a model cannot be presented from an authority outside ourselves, but must emerge from within, through eyes open to a new vision. This is the crux of the message in these verses at the end of Genesis 3, when Eve is finally named. Here her disruptive essence ushers in the new image of humanity, an image that we will, from here on, continually reshape and remold.

Her image as a mother brings up an essential aspect of motherhood. One of the most powerful ways we establish connection with others, especially infants—a connection that is then reactivated through every social interaction for the rest of our lives—is through touch. Touch is essential for family bonding, which eventually extends to social bonding. It has been proved that babies can die if they are not touched. From loving touch we derive our deepest feelings of trust, which give us not only pleasure, but also comfort when we are in pain, hope when we despair, and that indispensable sense that we are not alone in this world but instead are connected, an integral element in the web of life.

The activity of touch builds powerful neural networks in the brain and, when touch is pleasurable, initiates our awareness of trust. It is usually our mother who begins this process with us as she rocks us, nurtures us, and attends to us with affection. She is, therefore, the prime coordinator of our awareness of love and of our potential for developing trusting and integrated psyches and societies. This type of social interaction deeply affects the shape of our awareness.

The simple social activity of touch affects hormones in the hypothalamus that stimulate the pituitary to produce growth hormones.

Affection, therefore, has an enormous impact on the brain's, and body's, growth patterns. A lack of affectionate touch can cause the brain to produce glucocortisoids. Scientific experiments prove that too much exposure to glucocortisoids can kill hormones in the hippocampus. This affects learning and memory by impairing cognitive and memory skills.

Affection is therefore a very powerful brain stimulant. It decreases stress, which not only germinates hormones that produce growth, but enhances cognitive and memory skills as well. It is the neurology of trust that has made us so adaptable, so intelligent, and so creative. We can no longer afford to minimize our capacities to both give and receive tenderness and sensitivity, those capacities that build the fibers of trust and enhance the neurology of cognition and memory. And we must realize that love, sexuality, and awareness are part of a much larger movement that is spiritual at its core and has been since the beginning of our humanity, when this tale started. All of this is inherent in Esha's new name, Hhevah, the mother of all living, the inner germ of all possible possibilities.

She is about to take on her most important task, conceiving and birthing Cain, who is not the villain he has been made out to be, but is instead that most adored being, the hero-son.

Return with the Elixir

Genesis 4 narrates the culmination of the hero's journey, exemplified by the actions of Cain, whose task is stated in a riddle in verse 7 (naturally, for the number 7 represents the principle of indetermination):

> *If thou doest well, shalt thou not*
> *be accepted? and if thou doest not well,*
> *sin lieth at the door. And unto*
> *thee shall be his desire, and thou shalt*
> *rule over him.*
>
> GENESIS 4:7

In its final sentence, this is very similar to the riddle given Esha in chapter 3.

According to Joseph Campbell, every hero journeys into the unknown to retrieve a restorative elixir, an *integrative* element, because the inner journey being portrayed is from incompleteness to wholeness. For example, in *Star Wars,* Luke Skywalker is a recognizable mytholog-ical archetype: the bored farm boy who ventures off into the unknown, unites with the princess, and saves the universe. In this metaphor of his own psychological journey to wholeness, the restorative elixir or inte-grative element is recognition. He discovers his lost opposite, the feminine, in the mythological form of the princess, and reintegrates her into his internal life in order to save his inner universe from the rigid forces of static control and destruction.

The hero's journey is a metaphor of our psychological life, the soul's life, which is everyone's internal life. Genesis, when interpreted mythologically, offers us a vision of feminine power integrated with masculine power, and Joseph Campbell helps us see how this is accomplished. "The material of myth is the material of our environment, . . ." Campbell offers in *Transformations of Myth through Time*. On the page facing those words is a photograph of a woman cradling an infant, a benign smile glowing on her youthful face. "This woman with her baby is the basic image of mythology," he asserts, ". . . the first experience of anybody is the mother's body."* Though most of us do not remember this experience consciously, it is indelibly imprinted upon the psyche. In this section of Genesis, Cain, Hhevah's son, completes the central image of the Madonna.

In the New Testament the image of the Madonna has remained intact. In the Genesis myth, however, mother and child—Eve and Cain—have both been vilified. Yet they are unmistakably central characters of the story. If we open up our inner eyes and see Eve and Cain mythologically, they become archetypes in the human psyche and represent powerful opposing, yet integrated, forces.

I have a friend named Suzy, whom I've known most of my life. Tragically, her husband died soon after their son was born. His death was due to a terrible disease brought on in part by his overindulgence in drugs. He was a successful businessman; no one would have suspected he had an addiction. Even Suzy didn't discover it until they had been married for several years. She is now convinced that denial—both hers and her husband's—played a huge role in his affliction and death. Consequently, Suzy has become a woman who is, in her own words, "ruthless for the truth." Cain—the main character in Genesis 4— embodies Suzy's realization. According to the Qabalah, his name,

---

*Joseph Campbell, *Transformations of Myth through Time* (New York: Harper and Row, 1990), 1.

Qof-Yod-final Noun,100.10.700, means "slayer of illusion," because he unfolds a cosmic 700, all possible possibilities, the Holy Grail sought by the principle of indetermination. Coupled with Qof and Yod, this is a powerful equation. Qof (100) is Aleph in duration and Yod (10) is individual form. Cain, therefore, is the fulfillment of all the processes so far delineated. He is, in fact, the bearer of light, and it is always inner light that slays illusions.

There's an old joke about a man who's lost his keys. He's looking under a streetlight for them when a passerby walks up and asks, "What are you doing?" The man replies, "Looking for my keys." The passerby asks, "Is this where you lost them?" The man says, "No, but the light is better here." This is a joke that we intuitively know is about us, about the brain's processes of interpreting information. It isn't outer light that saves us; it is inner light.

An ability to slay illusion must be generated from within the psyche as we labor for integration, wholeness, and clarity because *perception* is the foundation of self-awareness and autonomy. This includes, first and foremost, knowledge of ourselves, of the way the brain processes information. The ability to maintain clarity by slaying illusions in our minds is the elixir we must return with on our hero's journey if we wish to be happy and whole. Our instrument of perception is ourselves. If we do not perceive directly, knowing that we are the Revelation of life, why do we not check our instrument instead of looking for truth with inadequate means?

In this sense, all inner journeys are the same because they all seek clarity. Yet, paradoxically, each journey is unique because of the specific illusions slain in order to gain that clarity.

One of the illusions I had to slay during my own journey was my belief that I didn't need affection or reassurance. It was an illusion I'd carried since childhood: I'd never had enough affection to give me the feeling of being loved and accepted, so as a child I'd developed the attitude of thinking I didn't need to be loved. My therapist said that was a good strategy at the time because it helped me survive. But as an adult it hindered my search for wholeness. Once I had married and realized my husband was not affectionate enough to reassure me that he loved me, I had to learn to ask for affection. It was a difficult process, largely because of my own built-in resistance to asking, which made me feel vulnerable. I had to work very hard to overcome that resistance, just as Cain, in this story, must work to overcome his.

His resistance is representative of the way patriarchy undermines our struggles for wholeness by insisting that God is the only authority in our lives, represented by high religious figures such as the pope. In this part of Genesis, Cain must overcome his resistance to actualizing autonomy. The idea that God is an authority outside ourselves is an illusion that is simply not true psychologically. Cain, then, represents our deepest psychological actions to become fully autonomous by challenging the notion of who God is and, conversely, who we are.

The illusion that the power of God resides outside us somewhere and that high religious men embody his authority—a pattern re-created in almost every aspect of patriarchal culture, from the hierarchy of governments and corporations to the hierarchy of the family—is still being challenged today. It is a pattern constantly foisted on us during our social interactions and during the processing of symbols used in literacy. (How many books are being written and published in which *he* is still the dominant pronoun?)

Cain's task is to slay the illusion at the root of the patriarchal pattern: that the power of God is outside us and that the image of God is male. As the slayer of illusion, or the bearer of light, however you wish to think of it, he is the archetype who returns with the elixir and recovers self-empowerment. He also guards against any attempt to dilute it, thereby ensuring that our inner awareness assumes the role of authority in our life. Inner awareness is crucial to autonomy; if we are to be whole, awareness must grow strong and powerful, because it is the essential element in the YHWH pattern of being.

FATHERS ABOVE, FATHERS BELOW

*And Adam knew Eve his wife; and she
conceived, and bare Cain, and said, I
have gotten a man from YHWH.*

GENESIS 4:1

Though this is generally overlooked, the manner in which Cain is conceived is very similar to the conception of Jesus in the New Testament. Adam is Eve's husband but he is not the father of Cain, just as Joseph is not the father of Jesus, although he is Mary's husband. Eve conceives Cain through YHWH, a Qabalic acronym that refers to the supreme integrative pattern. As we have seen, it represents the integration of inner life with outer life, a mutually fertilizing arrangement that can occur only in human beings and which perpetuates psychological, intellectual, and spiritual growth. YHWH is *not* a disembodied deity, but rather the pattern of integration for our own potential.

Several hundred years after Genesis was written, Mary conceived her son Jesus the same way Cain is conceived in Genesis, through YHWH, not her husband. The husbands, it seems, are necessary to the stories, but not for the all-important conception of the hero-sons, who are both slayers of illusion. Both husbands were the witnesses to the fertilization of the inner feminine by the pattern of YHWH.

The second verse of Genesis 4 goes on to say that ". . . she again bare his brother Abel. And Abel was a keeper of sheep, but Cain was a tiller of the ground." Abel's birth, as it is narrated in the Bible, is very different from Cain's, though that fact seems to have escaped traditional interpreters. Not only is there no mention of Adam knowing his wife intimately—witnessing the fertilization—but also YHWH is not mentioned as the fertilizing agent. Further, the descriptions of what each brother becomes are quite different: Abel is defined as a "keeper of sheep," whereas Cain is designated a "tiller of the ground."

These are the critical differences between the two brothers, who are not historical people but archetypes of male energy in the psyche. Earlier in the story, Adam is supposed to till the ground, meaning Adamah. Later, when he is cursed, he is told that he will become the dust from which he has been formed and that all the work he will do in the ground will be done by the sweat of his labor. Finally, Adam is sent from the garden to till Adamah, whence he came.

And now Cain is being designated as a "tiller of the ground." He is being recognized, in this verse, as the only one who finally accomplishes the task that Adam was originally directed to perform. He has, in other words, inherited the best of Adam's masculine characteristics, though Adam is not his father, just as Jesus is characterized as "the carpenter's son," though Joseph (the carpenter) is not his father. The reason these sons have inherited such characteristics from their non-fathers is that they represent enlightened masculine archetypes engaged in the all-important process of supporting and protecting the feminine goal of neural integration by slaying the illusions that prevent it.

The linguistic imagery of mythology often has the uncanny ability to sum up our psychological states. Take, for instance, the Greek myth of Narcissus, the story of a beautiful young man who falls in love with his own image. Though we are familiar with this story, we do not normally associate it with patriarchy. Yet Narcissus is precisely the image of patriarchy because patriarchy is the state of men in love with the power of their own masculinity. They have not yet learned to recognize and integrate the power of the feminine, so they are beautiful but incomplete.

I have a friend who, as I write this, is struggling with the issue of power within her marriage. She has been in a difficult relationship for the past several years and is coming to grips with how it developed. Lately she has begun to realize how unhappy she has been and has been considering where she might turn for guidance. She has recently been contemplating the wisdom of various religious and spiritual groups that claim to have answers for such confusing issues.

A few nights ago she had a particularly vivid dream in which she was in a room with several leaders of various religious organizations, all men, of course. All were patriarchal: The pope was there; along with a Sufi teacher; a Zen monk; Muhammad, the founder of Islam; a rabbi; a Roman Catholic priest; and various representatives of smaller religious offshoots, such as the Mormons and Jehovah's Witnesses. Suddenly, a tall man in flowing robes burst into the room and, with a sweeping motion of his arm that included all those austere figures present, declared, "No one is enlightened!" He then turned and abruptly left, slamming the door behind him. That figure was my friend's inner Cain, slaying her illusion that someone else, some person in a position of religious authority, knew what she should do to be happy. By slaying the illusion, he brings light to awareness.

Abel is the embodiment of all patriarchal illusions, especially those concerning power and authority and the social patterns that become established because of such assumptions. When Cain slays Abel, rather than slaying a person, he is slaying such illusions. In my friend's dream, Abel is exemplified by all the religious leaders who continually convey the illusion that the power of God is outside the self, a power that can be mediated only by chosen or self-appointed male representatives. Cain, if activated, will destroy that illusion and reinstate power to the self, because that is his sacred function.

My own observations have led me to the conclusion that patriarchy is a pattern using domination and obedience as basic elements of relationships because the unaware male psyche sees relationships as hierarchical, beginning with the relationship an individual has with God. The patriarchal pattern is based on the notion that God is above us and demands obedience. This idea originates with traditional interpretations of the Genesis myth. Such ideas, I believe, are peculiar aspects of men's psyches when they have not been integrated. Domination and obedience diminish and devalue the role of trust and mutual respect in relationships, beginning with that between men and women in marriage.

Within the relationship of marriage, when women are subjected to the whims of patriarchal men and are put in the position of being hierarchically lower and of less value than men, all types of domination and betrayal are committed between partners and are passed on to their children. This powerful illusion of men's superiority to women forms the basis of our current social patterns. It is the flat Earth belief that we still live by, in this symbolic seventh day of cultural conditioning. But when Cain slays Abel, he is not only slaying the idea that God lies somewhere outside the self; he is also slaying this idea that men are superior to women, the central pattern of patriarchy.

Cain is the only one who can slay this pattern; because men have created it, men must end it. The only men capable of ending it, however, are sons conceived from YHWH, hero-sons, which each of us becomes as we slay those illusions around us that are inherent in patriarchy, thereby paving the way for autonomy. This is how we remove the logs from our eyes and learn to see with clarity.

My friend who had the dream, I'll call her Nancy, has been unhappy in her relationship because her spouse has acted in ways that alienate her, through typical male dominance behaviors that I have labeled "the gorilla factor." When angry, his anger has been accompanied by what she perceives as threatening actions, such as thumping his fist on the table. In the past, when she tried to make him aware of this, his response was to become even angrier and then end the discussion. She has finally gained the courage to tell him she no longer wishes to live with these behaviors, and if they split up because of her decision, it's okay with her. She is reinstating her power. Until now, she felt disempowered, but because she is clear about what she wants, her power is returning. She has regained clarity by slaying illusions such as the belief that to create a happy marriage she had to suppress her own needs and support her husband's, a typical patriarchal pattern. Her growth toward autonomy means realizing that what she really wants is a happy self and that she may have to end a bad marriage to recover it.

At this point, Nancy and her husband are still together because he has finally realized that he does not want to lose her and is willing to change to meet her newly realized needs. They are now both engaged in a reeducation process, teaching themselves healthier ways to relate and communicate with one another. Their relationship is growing and changing and they are both confused and excited by this, and willing to keep working. I have great hopes for them.

In a society such as ours, where external powers are the ones recognized as legitimate, the hero's journey to wholeness is often perceived as worthless. Yet if we, as individuals, do not embark upon this inner journey, we can never be happy, no matter how much outer power we may accumulate—academic degrees, wealth, status, fame, and so on—because we still won't be powerful or clear in our own internal world. Any feelings of worthlessness, powerlessness, lack of approval, lack of love, and so forth, that are active in our internal world will continually sabotage any accomplishments we may attain in the outer world. Those feelings can be addressed only through the inner journey. Deny those feelings and you run the risk of being subject to addictions, neuroses, or abusive, hurtful relationships, to name but a few of the consequences.

THE NEUROCHEMISTRY OF WHOLENESS

Based on the assumption that God wants to dominate us and that we must, in natural consequence, obey him, the institutionalization of patriarchy has legitimized certain domination behaviors in social interactions. This is the way the neocortex perceives the situation. The stress induced by such attitudes creates neurochemistries that have an enormous impact on the psyche. A major point of Genesis is to wrest our thinking from the grip of the neocortex's limited vision of reality because it includes absolutely no awareness of the inner world of the psyche.

Dominance—a pattern that animals use to create and maintain their social hierarchies—produces a specific neurochemical result in the human brain, one that has been repeated for over 260 million years. One of the neurochemical results of dominance is the suppression of healthy serotonin levels—a major neurotransmitter that deals with mood. It has recently been discovered that our levels of serotonin are often set during childhood, and that these levels depend upon the degree of stress a child experiences in family and social interactions. If early family interactions are based on trust and mutual respect, which produce the least stress in relationships, they will generate happiness and fun, balanced with responsibility and discipline. Once healthy serotonin levels are set, a child can continue in life with healthy attitudes, moods, and activities.

If, however, our family and social interactions are characterized by the stress of dominance, obedience, humiliation, and other patriarchal patterns, we will likely develop feelings of insecurity, shame, anger, confusion, and so forth, and serotonin will be set at unhealthy levels. Such family dynamics are reinforced by cultural patterns. One of the central messages of Christianity is that we are all sinners. Such a message is destructive, psychologically, keeping us locked into patterns of incompleteness while allowing religious authorities to manipulate our serotonin levels and, through our own neurochemistry, to control us. We are then "captured" in an unhealthy neurochemical feedback loop in our own brains, a situation that lends itself to thinking that we are being punished for our sins. This feedback loop, and the stress it will continually reproduce, is something many of us will intuitively recognize as unhealthy and seek to change at some point.

A short time ago, I watched a disturbing program on the Discovery Channel about young men and violence in which a group of four youths, ages sixteen to eighteen, were videotaping themselves as they drove around in a stolen car, bashing parked cars with a baseball bat. The damage began to escalate until they began bashing people with the bat—a man riding a bicycle, a woman standing at a bus stop. Later, they were apprehended, and when the police confiscated their videotape and watched it, the voices of the young men could be heard commenting on their violent activities as they were executing them. One of the boys said something like, "Whenever I feel down on myself, I just go out and bash. It picks me back up."

Bad feelings often develop because our social environment projects bad feelings onto us, especially when we are children unable to defend ourselves. They come in messages such as: "You'll never amount to any-thing; you're worthless trash" and "Why can't you think straight?" and "If you want something to cry about, I'll give you something to cry about!" The psyche is bombarded with verbal messages designed to dominate and humiliate. As children we have no defense against such domination tactics, so we "take them on," and may even model them in our own behavior. But they are so unhealthy psychologically that we attempt to throw them off, often in antisocial ways, like the boys' bash-ing behavior. What such feelings require is the opposing perspective: "You are valuable. You matter. You have enormous potential to change"—all statements of trust and respect. Such counteracting state-ments, along with appropriate affectionate behavior, can neutralize the violence in "feeling bad" about oneself.

Many of us experienced childhood traumas such as emotional abandonment and neglect, which are forms of psychological violence. Like the bashing boys, many of us have not learned to identify our unhealthy feelings, so we pass them along in strange passive or aggres-sive ways and they continue on, unrecognized. These negative or destructive feelings generated during childhood trauma have deep neu-rochemical roots and usually continue to be active in our adult lives, though we may deny them, which can lead to addictions, neuroses, dys-functions, violence, and breakdowns.

This is Cain's battleground because such feelings and negativity are integral to the personal and social patterns of patriarchy. When we gen-erate our own Cain, our slayer of illusion, we reclaim our alienated needs for tenderness and affection that domination had banished to the basement of our psyche. In recognizing that our childhood wounds may still need to be healed, we can then be open to suggestions for methods of integration, accepting and embracing our vulnerabilities. This creates new neurochemical patterns and begins the healing process that leads to wholeness.

Within the brain, as within society, the power base of external authority is usually some form of domination and the neurochemistry it promotes. The Cinderella story provides a good illustration of this pattern. In it, the stepfamily uses domination to keep Cinderella in servitude. In our social interactions, anger is one specific domination tactic used by people to keep others "in line," because it involves a threat of violence. Another tactic is to tell someone he or she is bad, useless, stupid, or ugly; and still another is to designate people "inferior" based on race. But such threatening, alienating tactics can never build strong social or psychological bonds because they have as their basis the neurochemistry of fear and anxiety. We cannot feel close to people when our neurochemistry is telling us to fear them. The strongest social bonds develop during interactions that promote responsibility, tenderness, trust, and love because the underlying neurochemistry inherent in such interactions makes us feel good about ourselves and those to whom we are relating. We want to be close to them. This is healthy and promotes continued growth.

Such positive traits are often defined as angelic. Yet they are meant to form the basis of the simple interactions between mothers and infants, parents and children, and among citizens in a society. Interactions of trust and mutual respect that come from these traits generate a neurochemistry much different from that induced by domination behaviors.

In the myth of Genesis, obedience (the forerunner of domination) is challenged by Esha and the dominance patterns of assumed outer authority are challenged by Cain, who must destroy the illusion that such patterns have validity in human social interactions. Each of these challenges generates a new neurochemical pattern in the brain. Human beings have the potential to rise above the hierarchical social patterns developed by animals and to integrate new neurochemistries. Love, tolerance, respect, trust, insight, and foresight—and the behaviors these neurochemistries generate—transform and transfigure old evolutionary patterns in the brain and culture (which may originate in the older cortexes) through the integrative agenda of the frontal lobes.

Most addiction recovery processes as well as most emotional and spiritual healing therapies are based on reintegrating our own inner power base to produce a specific type of neurochemistry. Self-empowerment, in turn, "slays" the idea that power lies elsewhere—in the bottle, in the drug, in holding political office or being CEO, or in an external God, which are all maintained through the old neurochemical patterns of fear, anxiety, and dominance.

This is the heart of events taking place in the final chapter of the Genesis myth: the realization of the psyche's endowed power, which in turn generates the neurochemical patterns of self-empowerment, trust, and respect. Such neurochemistry has powerful effects. It can heal sickness and trauma. It can lead to personal growth and awareness. It can show us the way to autonomy. It can make new connections in the brain until it pervades our life, eventually producing happiness, love, and fulfillment.

This is our birthright, to live in this heaven, a heaven created through the neurochemistry of wholeness. After all, happy people do not blow up buildings, mow down their classmates with automatic weapons, abandon their spouses or children, molest or stalk, or engage in any number of other antisocial behaviors, all of which are accompanied by specific neurochemistries. Happy individuals generate happy families and happy societies without problems and without the need to spend billions solving those problems.

Happiness is the result of the neurochemistry of wholeness. By developing wholeness in the psyche, which releases its specific neurochemical pattern, we not only discover happiness for ourselves, but we also do our part to heal the social injustices we see around us.

OFFERINGS AND RIDDLES

And in the process of time it came to
pass, that Cain brought of the fruit of
the ground an offering unto the Lord.
And Abel, he also brought of the firstlings

of his flock and of the fat thereof. And the
Lord had respect unto Abel and to his offering:

But unto Cain and to his offering he had
not respect. And Cain was very wroth,
and his countenance fell.

GENESIS 4:3–5

In the hierarchical relationship that patriarchal man has with his (perceived) God, God is the ultimate outer source of power controlling all life. Such an ideology serves to diminish our awareness of the importance of how we relate to ourselves and others. This is the crux of the situation in which Cain finds himself. He gives an offering to YHWH that isn't accepted, yet Abel's offering is. What a curious riddle.

If we remember, however, that Cain and Abel are psychological archetypes, the riddle is solved. Cain, the slayer of illusion, is not living up to his title if he is making offerings to YHWH, because by making such offerings he is not honoring his own autonomy. Abel embodies the idea of the necessity of worshiping an external God. He can't even recognize an illusion, much less slay it. But Cain has become tangled up in Abel's ideology. Why is he, the bearer of light, bearing offerings? He has obviously forgotten who he is.

YHWH is not a vengeful God, but rather our own inner pattern of autonomy whispering in our mind. Such a possibility quietly asks the obvious: "Why are you wroth and why has your countenance fallen?"

If thou doest well, shalt thou not
be accepted? and if thou doest not well
sin lieth at the door. And unto
thee shall be his desire, and thou shalt
rule over him.

GENESIS 4:7

With this verse we circle back to the two pairs of opposites that have been driving this myth all along: continuity/certainty and disruption/possibilities. The words *doest well* and *doest not well* are similar in meaning to the words that describe the tree of the knowledge of *good and evil*. The key to solving this riddle is hidden in the equations of the sacred symbols, and can be lived only in freedom, for it is the key of life. Were it a commandment, Cain might obey it and thereby become his brother's keeper, losing his freedom and autonomy.

The riddle begins with the Qabalic formula Hay-Lammed-Vav-Aleph (5.30.6.1), which is similar to an opening statement. When this formula is solved in action within us, the revelation is present as an intuitive breakthrough. Cain comprehends it and acts accordingly. His mythological mission, that of God in exile, or humanity unaware of its true being and nature, is to give life (5), organic movement (30) and fertility (6) to Aleph (1). In other words, we, as indeterminate beings, are meant to allow Aleph to move in us so that we can fertilize our latent potential. "Thou doest well" is Aleph-Mem–Tav-Yod-Tayt-Yod-Bayt (1.40.400.10.9.10.2), describing what happens to Aleph when it cannot overcome the resistance of Mem (40). It becomes buried in cosmic resistance (400), in which the feminine power of organic construction is encased between two Yod (10.9.10) for the benefit of Bayt (2). This "doest well" is very misleading, and results in 300.1000.400, a Sheen (300) and an exalted Aleph (1000) hurling themselves against the obstinate resistance of 400. The standard translation is, "Shalt thou not be accepted?" The other formula, 6.1000.600, offers the alternative, a negation of "doest well," which we read as "doest not well."

The result is an extraordinary peace and flowering that is a dialogue between the brain's advanced neural structures and its most primitive. This is a deep penetration of awareness into consciousness. Remember, the authors of this text have an earnest suspicion of the static nature of *good*. To those authors, TVB/*good* is synonymous with stagnant, rigid, and continuous. They abhor it because it has been so unquestioningly embraced by patriarchal ideology. To the Qabalists, *good* is the worst illusion by which we can operate. Penetrating to the depths of consciousness releases us from the simple dichotomy of good and evil, of doing well and doing not well, which has no validity in a reality of perpetual growth. The freeing of all indeterminate potential occurs through the frontal lobes when they integrate the rest of the brain, which brings about new awareness.

This pattern, of integrating the self, is directly opposed to the old neocortical pattern of domination, inherited from patriarchal paradigms. To do well in that paradigm is to dominate, so to do not well is to integrate. That's the puzzle Cain solves. The sin that lies at the door is an opening, as all doors are.

EXISTENCE VS. LIFE

And Cain talked with Abel his brother:
and it came to pass, when they were in
the field, that Cain rose up against Abel
his brother, and slew him.

GENESIS 4:8

In the original Qabalic formulas, Cain is described as being raised above Abel, not the literal "rose up against." Qof-Vav-Mem (100.6.600) describes the cosmic fertility achieved in consciousness when Qof unites with Vav and final Mem. When that fertility is achieved, the consciousness that was Abel simply disintegrates. Cain, who has become the container of timeless life, slays illusion by penetrating veils in the mind. The slaying of an illusion is achieved by simply bathing in light an assumption or conflict. It is enlightenment that slays illusion, by clarifying details. Cain doesn't actually slay Abel. Cain, bearing his gift of light, penetrates consciousness, the darkness of assumption, of sacred cows, of obsolete beliefs, which Abel represents. Cain is an archetype in the psyche that demands we examine every thought, every concept, every theory, every belief, every ideology, every authority, and every symbol we currently embrace. This examination gives our brain the opportunity to see clearly and create new neurochemical patterns based on our own experience or insight, not on what someone else tells us or what others assume. If Cain does not operate this way, he has failed his mission. His purpose is to empower the self with clarity.

Cain represents the warrior protector in the frontal lobes. He is conceived through fertilization with YHWH and is meant to slay every illusion our minds mistakenly dream up.

Then YHWH—in order to make sure that Cain has learned his lesson—asks about Abel.

> *And YHWH said unto Cain, Where*
> *Is Abel, thy brother? And he said, I*
> *know not: Am I my brother's keeper?*
>
> GENESIS 4:9

This is a perfect reply from Cain, given the circumstances now revealed. He is assuredly not his brother's keeper, because his brother represents the static element of clinging to false ideology. How can Cain be the keeper of that? It would dishonor everything he represents.

Cain has merely shone his light, in which the illusion of Abel simply vanishes. The slaying is a metaphor about the pruning of our own neural networks, the ones carrying the information of illusion. We cut off such networks; just as we grow up and realize Santa isn't real, so we grow up and realize patriarchy and domination are inauthentic. Why would Cain care what happened to Abel? Abel was never valid.

> *And he said, What hast thou done? the*
> *voice of thy brother's blood crieth unto*
> *me from the ground [Adamah].*
>
> GENESIS 4:10

Notice that the blood has a voice that is crying from the ground. There is no wrath being directed toward Cain from YHWH. Abel's blood is crying to YHWH from the ground. That's the same ground Cain is tilling. It is the ground of awareness. Abel's blood is crying from it because his ideology is false and has therefore been reabsorbed within the ground of the psyche. Learning new truths often requires that we prune away old ideas. This learning, pruning, and recycling is the essence of transformation and involves intricate neurochemical changes through a vast network of the brain's neural channels and cortexes.

> *And now art thou cursed from the earth,*
> *which hath opened her mouth to receive*
> *thy brother's blood from thy hand.*

> *When thou tillest the ground, it shall*
> *not henceforth yield unto thee her strength;*
> *a fugitive and a vagabond shalt thou be*
> *in the earth.*

GENESIS 4:11–12

Notice that all those curses are originating from the earth, not from YHWH and not from Adamah. It is the earth that is now cursing Cain. In this sense the earth represents the generator of continuity and of the old neurochemistry of obedience and domination in our brain—that which has been inherited from evolution, encapsulated in the three oldest cortexes. The word *fugitive* is 50.6.70, Noun-Vav-Ayn. In colloquial Hebrew it means "to waver," in a great variety of ways. But from its formula we can see that this wavering is a perversion of the *instability* born of a fertilizing action, which is what the formula depicts: the life in forms (50) is fertile (6) and produces fecundity (70). The fact that this verse states that Cain is a fugitive in the earth means that his newly acquired fertile state is not inherited from the earth. He is not, henceforth, related to her and she will no longer yield unto him her strength. The word *strength* is an unused root, *kowach,* in Hebrew meaning "to be firm." The formula is Kaf-Vav-Hay (20.6.5). It depicts Kaf, the existence of a containing element (20), fertilized by (6), yielding life (5). This life of the container isn't really life, because it isn't begotten from Aleph.

The subtle difference between *existence* and *life* is being addressed here. The earth is the element of static continuity in existence that is represented by the three older cortexes. Earth is cursing Cain because he now allows his disruptive, dynamic nature to be active through the neurochemistry of wholeness, promoting growth and change in awareness. The strength the evolutionary earth will no longer yield to him is just that, her static nature. The frontal lobes are no longer tied to survival-of-the-fittest paradigms, but function through wisdom, love, and grace.

> *And Cain said unto YHWH, My*
> *punishment is more than I can bear.*
>
> *Behold, thou hast driven me out this*
> *day from the face of the earth; and from*
> *thy face shall I be hid; and I shall be a*
> *fugitive and a vagabond in the earth;*
> *and it shall come to pass, that every*
> *one that findeth me shall slay me.*
>
> GENESIS 4:13–14

When we Qabalically decode *punishment* (the literal Hebrew means "perversity"), we find that it means something very different from what we linguistically assume. The Qabalic acronym is AVVfN, Ayn-Vav-Vav-final Noun. It means that all indeterminate potential in individual form, Ayn (70), in a dual copulation, Vav and Vav (6 and 6), yields an incredible cosmic fertility, final Noun (700). The drama at the core of this myth is the function and transformation of the feminine, germ elements of disruption—specifically intuition, insight, and foresight and the neurochemical patterns they give birth to—in our processes of self-discovery and empowerment. With this acronym yielding a 700, that potential has been realized. The number of cosmic indetermination, all possible possibilities, is 700. The fact that Cain says that this state of fertility is more than he can *bear* reveals another hidden message. *Bear* is translated from the Hebrew *nasah*, a primitive root meaning "to lift." The acronymic formula is NSH, Noun-Sammekh-Hay, 50.60.5: The life of individual forms (50) and the fertility of individual forms (60) yields life (5). Cain is realizing his awesome potential. It lifts him out of mere mortal existence into the exalted life of ever becoming, the life of the soul, of wholeness.

He says that he has been driven out, this day, from the face of the (limited) earth, which is the face of static continuity in existence. And he is also *hidden* from the face of YHWH, meaning YHWH is now hidden within him and he can no longer project power to an outside source, nor can he supplicate it. Cain, like us, resists the prospect of being autonomous. It deprives him of his familiar though illusory comforts. There is no church he can belong to, no deity he can supplicate in times of distress. He is his own authority, driven from the element of continuity to which others cling. He has become a fugitive and a vagabond from rigid perspectives, and everyone who still clings to those values will slay him.

Now consider this: What happened to Martin Luther King Jr., to William Wallace (the Scottish hero depicted in the movie *Braveheart*), and to Joan of Arc, as well as countless others? Were they not slain and were not their deaths orchestrated by powers that did not want them disrupting a structure of social continuity that ensured power to an elite few?

Such power struggles take place in the psyche all the time, because of the brain's design. The oldest three cortexes—the r-complex, the limbic system, and the neocortex—engendered by the limitations of the "earth," embody the forces of continuity that continually seek to dominate our spirit of growth. Yet that tiny spirit (of David, of Cain, and of Hhevah) prevails—if we offer allegiance to it instead of to external power sources that seek to dominate us by manipulating the neuro-chemistries of the three lower cortexes.

Cain is the very image of timelessness itself, which is what disruption offers us. All ideologies based in continuity, therefore, seek to kill Cain. But Cain has finally recognized himself and has therefore immediately gained the recognition of YHWH.

> *And YHWH said unto him, Therefore*
> *whosoever slayeth Cain, vengeance shall*
> *be taken upon him sevenfold. And YHWH*
> *set a mark upon Cain, lest any finding him*
> *should kill him.*
>
> GENESIS 4:15

Knowing that Cain and Abel are archetypes in the psyche makes this last verse understandable. Cain is the element that slays all limiting illusions of continuity by bringing light into the depths of the psyche. Naturally he is going to be protected by YHWH. He is an absolute necessity to a healthy psychological life. "Sevenfold" refers to the unfolding of indeterminate potential, the quest of all life.

> *And Cain went out from the presence*
> *of YHWH, and dwelt in the Land of*
> *Nod, on the east of Eden.*
>
> GENESIS 4:16

This is the verse that recognizes exactly who Cain is, because it shows him residing in the east, where the timeless tree of life is, because that is where he is supposed to live. We are supposed to live there too, along with Cain, because *living* is what we are supposed to be doing, not merely surviving in a continuous static pattern of existence. Authentic living requires regular doses of timelessness and disruption, change and transformation, play and experimentation. These forces birth a new neurochemistry of self-trust in the brain; this is what the tree of life provides in its exotic fruit.

Cain has achieved his goal: slaying the limiting illusions concerning continuity, domination, and outer, hierarchical symbols of power. So he goes to live east of Eden, home of the timeless tree of life that engenders the authentic pattern of wholeness through a transforming new neurochemical pattern in the brain. He has earned his right to be there. He has challenged every concept and belief and, in the timeless process, found himself. Now he is the element in the psyche that recognizes no power base other than his own awareness of the timeless patterns of life itself. A mind that understands Cain is free at last from all illusions and is immersed, instead, in cosmic truth.

To See or Not to See

There's a little village on the high plains of Colombia that is the subject of the book *Gaviotas: A Village to Reinvent the World,* by journalist Alan Weisman. This community of some two hundred families has been living the life of the future for thirty years, a life fueled by technological innovation and the whole-systems pattern. Amid the war-torn landscape of Colombia's drug cartels, isolated by its rugged terrain, Gaviotas continues to thrive, reinventing the world at a slower pace and through life's timeless cycle, stated simply as this: The emissions produced by all natural systems—whether carbon, oxygen, nitrogen, or something else—are used to fuel other systems. This is why nature never makes a mess. Human beings, on the other hand, in the last three hundred years of industrialization, have organized industrial systems creating emissions that are not used as fuel for other systems, so they pollute. In fact, all pollution originates from this one flaw, this inability to see how the whole systems of nature function and using that model to generate those systems that we create.

Gaviotas is a village that works according to the pattern and cycle of nature. Gaviotans get their water using pumps they designed themselves that are installed in teeter-totters, so when the children play they simultaneously pump water for the village. It's ingenious, and so simple. The Gaviotans also install their pumps with windmills specially designed to capture the energy in lazy tropical breezes typical of their climate. When cattle come to water at the pumps, their manure is collected in chutes and directed to large vats. There it breaks down, producing methane, which is used to run equipment. Gaviotans produce all their own energy and food, designing equipment and integrated systems as need arises. They refuse to patent any of their inventions and instead give away the information to any who desire it. This is the model for the future, if we want to live happy, healthy, creative lives. The latest triumph for the Gaviotans is that they have planted over one million trees on thirty thousand acres, providing a new environment in which ancient dormant seeds of the rain forest have now sprouted. These will eventually reforest the high desert the community occupies.

Gaviotans have reinvented the human world through the ageless pattern of the natural world: whole systems. This is what we all must do eventually if we wish to create societies that are sustainable. If you would like to learn more about the development of whole systems, the Web site www.zeri.org has this information, along with news of experimental projects worldwide.

In 1994 an experiment was begun in a prison in India run by Kiran Bedi, the first female prison warden in that country. She wanted to find a way to get at the root of why so many men end up in prison. One of her guards suggested an ancient meditation practice called Vipasana. After consulting with a Vipasana teacher, who informed her that unless the guards understood Vipasana it would do no good for prisoners to attempt it, Kiran Bedi arranged for a group of prison guards to take a course in the practice. Once the guards had completed the course, she made arrangements for prisoners to take it, and in this way the largest Vipasana course ever conducted was held in her prison, Tihar Jail, in April 1994, with one thousand inmates participating.

Vipasana courses are conducted worldwide following the same format: Each course is ten days long and requires total silence. Practitioners sit silently with only one objective: to focus on the patch of skin beneath the nose. During the first three days of this silent exercise, the mind screams with all sorts of images, sounds, emotions, memories, dreams, illusions, wishes, denials, whatever. But on the fourth day, it quiets. Then, the little patch of skin becomes supersensitive. It can feel the subtlest flow of air. A new level of awareness and sensitivity opens because the brain is actually growing new neurons. The smallest sensations bombard the awareness: itchiness, tingling, heat, pressure—all natural, physical sensations experienced more vividly than ever before because the new neurons are creating feedback loops.

At the core of Vipasana practice is continued awareness of these subtle physical sensations without reacting to them. The brain produces neurons of awareness only, without any accompanying behavior. In this way, the old patterns between brain and behavior are interrupted and disrupted by these new patterns of awareness alone. Every sound, every vision, taste, smell, every sensation that the body experiences instantly produces a sensation of awareness. The technique focuses on these natural, physical sensations as the crucial link between mind and body, the key to understanding human behavior through self-observation. Through Vipasana, we may realize that our own attitudes and addictions, suffering and happiness are not caused by the outside world. States of awareness are reactions to pleasant or unpleasant sensations the world evokes in the body, which then dictate action and condition the mind through repetition. Students learn to objectively observe all the sensations in their body, whatever they may be, without reacting to them. They watch emotions come and go, watch pleasure come and go, watch pain come and go, and they realize—not intellectually, but through this concrete experience—that nothing is permanent. Hatred, passion, greed—these are not abstract anymore. By watching the physical sensations accompanying these emotions, and by understanding their impermanent nature, we can actually start changing the habit of blind reaction, the old neural networks in the brain that have had no intermediary awareness.

The men at Tihar Jail discovered that between the two poles of expression and suppression lies a third option: self-observation. The prisoners had the first real look at their inner world. They cried, they felt ashamed and guilty. They realized they had caused hurt to others, to themselves, and to society. They wanted to change and they wanted forgiveness. This was Kiran Bedi's intention. Her recidivism rate began to decline. Within three weeks Tihar Jail began to offer regular Vipasana courses.

Several studies on children have come to an interesting conclusion: Boys' brains are designed to react to the world, while girls' brains are designed to analyze it. We could conclude that the world is being run by reactionary males, but the deeper implications are more distressing. How do we educate ourselves to this awesome instrument inside our heads that contains the keys to our self-understanding and our ability to change behaviors that have a toxic consequence, whether it is higher murder rates or industrial pollution?

The brain is an information-processing instrument. It has learned to process the information in literacy. But it must also learn to process the information of self-awareness. This is the only way to become fully human.

To be fully human is to be angelic, wise, fun, and creative. The truth of authentic human nature and the neurochemistry of self-empowerment is that we are capable of enormous change. This neurochemistry is powered by germ energy—the feminine, self-generative, and disruptive potentials and possibilities of the mind and psyche—located in the frontal lobes of the human brain. To deny those powers is to deny the best, most authentic thing about us.

We have enormous, untapped potential. We cannot see it, touch it, taste it, hear it, or smell it; it cannot be perceived with our five recognized senses. Only when we open our *inner* eyes can we perceive this awesome gift and begin to shape it into the human journey of awareness that leads to wholeness. Learning to see through insight does much of the work of integration. It builds neural bridges in the brain and psyche, and eventually in our social interactions by birthing a new neurochemical pattern of trust in the brain.

I bumped into my friend Lily at the farmer's market the other day, and she told me a story about a recent experience she'd had that illustrates the power of learning to see, revealing how it integrates both the brain and psyche and heals life's imbalances.

Several months ago Lily came down with a blinding migraine, something she'd never experienced before. Her usual response to bodily discomfort is simply to ignore it, hoping it will go away. But after three days of unbearable pain, Lily finally went to the local immediate care facility. All she wanted was a prescription for pain pills so she could go to sleep at night and get enough rest to resume her normal activities during the day.

Instead of giving her the prescription, however, the doctor she happened to end up with began questioning her. "Are there any unusual stresses in your life right now?" he gently probed. Astonishingly, Lily burst into tears, something else she rarely does. She began telling him about her feelings concerning her work, which she used to love, but now, for some strange reason, was beginning to dread, so much so that she was considering changing careers. They talked for a while and when she left, she had no prescription for pain pills but was feeling much better anyway. Her migraine had diminished considerably. Her old neurochemistry about loyalties to her job was beginning to be dismantled.

While driving home, Lily continued thinking about her dilemma concerning work. Suddenly, a new thought disrupted her awareness. It came instantly, seemingly from out of nowhere, through that special neurochemistry in the frontal lobes that brings insight and intuition. Lily realized she had been working so hard that she had neglected her relationships with women friends whom she cherished. Feelings that had been repressed for months flooded into her awareness. She began to cry, realizing how much she missed the simple and fun company of her female companions. She resolved to renew her friendships and to always remember how valuable they are in her life.

It was then that her migraine vanished completely, because the neurochemistry that prompted it had been addressed through awareness. She has since initiated a tradition of gathering with her friends for a weekend at a cabin on the Mendocino coast, simply to be together, play, have fun, and celebrate their friendships as women. Through feeding and nourishing a neurochemistry that she had been neglecting, Lily now continually regenerates it so that it adds to her life of fullness.

If Lily had received her desired prescription for pain pills (substituting an outside source of neurochemical change instead of building an inner one), she may never have had her realization. She is thankful for that wise doctor. This is how we learn to see, by probing the sources of our discomfort until insight shows us the way to wholeness, healing, and integration.

By forming an allegiance with the frontal lobes' agenda of integration, we initiate the germination of new neurons, synapses, and neurochemistries in our brain that eventually connect all the other cortexes, creating wholeness. Only by creating this wholeness—which eventually disarms the egoistic, denial, and dominance apparatus in the brain—will we be able to overcome the immense obstacles to be faced in the future. Without minds that are unified, there is no possibility of permanent peace on this planet or even of simple happiness for individuals.

The human psyche is a monumental driving force in all our lives. It desires self-knowledge and unity, which are attained only through personal, psychological, and spiritual growth. That growth is the result of an interplay between opposites, as we integrate outer behavior with inner awareness, generating new neurons, new neural networks, and new neurochemistries in the brain. This new neural landscape produces unity by weaving all the separate pieces and cortexes of the brain together through insight, under the direction of the frontal lobes.

Without exception, all of us are either on this journey of integration or waiting to begin it.

The human psyche, though it has enormous potential, is also incalculably fragile. If it is damaged in any way, especially during childhood, that damage will continue to reveal itself throughout our life, though we may try valiantly to deny and hide it. By continually revealing its own damage and neurochemical imbalances, the psyche's intent is to find healing. A failure to produce that healing, which restores psychological unity and wholeness, is by far the biggest drain on our gross national product, more than any other single item.

The cost of mitigating domination behaviors, denial, addictions, dysfunctions, and violence caused by our lack of personal psychological unity is staggering, much more than we can even begin to measure. A few spectacular events are but the tip of the dysfunctional human iceberg: the bombing of the Federal Building in Oklahoma, the Columbine (and other school) shootings, continual unrest in the Middle East, and the monumental tragedies of September 11. Such sad and baffling circumstances can be healed through self-awareness and self-empowerment in frontal lobe development using a recognition of the pattern of cosmic wholeness, the original basis of all religions and all spiritual practices. We must, however, reclaim our inner growth processes from religious practices that continue to focus the mind on an outer God.

The word *health* originates from a German word that means "whole," and is as applicable to our neural states—mental, spiritual, and psychological—as it is to our biological state. The sacred code in Genesis is the ultimate story of wholeness, uniting cosmological and biological evolution with psychological, spiritual, and cultural evolution, through symbols that convey the reality of a dynamic occurring everywhere between pairs of opposites as they express that wholeness.

For the individual, that pair is psyche and behavior, inner and outer. YHWH is the Qabalic symbol representing that fertilizing interplay within us. Until we learn to see how our behavior affects the environment, culture, and those around us and how our inner neurochemisty of beliefs, mind-sets, paradigms, and intentions affects our behavior, we will be blind, no matter how many technological marvels we might invent. It is this inner blindness that will, if not awakened, eventually destroy us. Opening our inner eyes and seeing accurately the contents of our own psyche and the real consequences of our actions is the ultimate challenge for humanity.

Every story told is told by the human psyche, which is the ultimate storyteller. And every psyche tells the vision of itself, its own becoming or its own stagnation, as the case may be. The story you've just read—the myth of Genesis—is a hero's journey of neural integration. Through it we learn that the potential and desire to connect, integrate, and manifest wholeness, whether emotionally, psychologically, or spiritually, is promoted by feminine, nurturing, mothering energy originating from a frontal lobe agenda. We need more of this connecting energy in our lives to heal and soothe the separation and loneliness that plague us in our patriarchal, compartmentalized, and fragmented illusions.

Adam is the intellect who finally recognizes feminine power and objective as integrative, and who therefore betrays his own tendencies toward domination in order to support his feminine partner. Eve is the archetype who sees the pattern of interacting opposites that is the foundation of wholeness and undertakes the task of integrating the opposing forces of continuity/time and disruption/timelessness. Cain is the hero-son who protects the fragile possibility of wholeness forever by shining the light of awareness that slays all illusions of separation, thereby keeping us connected to our own internal power source, the trustworthy compass of wholeness that guides us on our journey through life.

The secret dowry that is buried within each of us is the psyche's germ that has the potential to grow indefinitely until we discover all of life's riches, especially happiness, healing, love, and wisdom. This germ is the power to see and recognize the integrative pattern of life as the interplay between opposites. Like Adam and Eve, each of us must eat and digest the fruit of the tree of the knowledge of TVB and RA, transforming its misbegotten interpretation of good and evil. In that transformation we discover that it is actually the fruit of the tree of the knowledge of sacred opposites, the basis of wholeness. This is the truth that opens our eyes and sets us free to view life in a whole new way.

Appendix 1

Studying the Qabalah

One way we become enculturated is through language. The Qabalah offers us a language that is completely outside the box of culture. Learning it expands the mind's awareness beyond the cultural paradigms by which we normally operate. The Qabalah offers, in a word, transcendence. Studying it is a rigorous, tedious undertaking, but its rewards are enlightenment and awareness of the universal patterns of life.

In order to study the Qabalah, you need to know the Hebrew spellings of the words in Genesis. There are several ways to obtain this information. Any canonized Hebrew version of Genesis will do. But remember, Hebrew is written from right to left, as opposed to English, which is written from left to right, and you must train yourself to read any Hebrew text this way. To read the original Hebrew spellings in Genesis, I used Strong's *The Exhaustive Concordance of the Bible,* which can be purchased from any Christian Science Reading Room for about twenty dollars. Ask the attendant to show you how to use it to look up Hebrew translations of English words. Another way is to enter "Gateway to the Qabalah" on your search engine. On the page that appears, click on "Bible Searches." The database for Strong's *Concordance* can be found on this site. There are probably other Web sites with this information as well.

After you find the Hebrew spellings of the English words, you must translate each Hebrew letter according to the Autiot of the Qabalah, the definitions of which can be found in the chart on page 200. It's important to understand that the meaning of the Qabalah lies in *relationships.* It can be studied using only the numbers and their relationships to each other, but the words—Aleph, Bayt, and so on—are necessary to apply the Qabalah to the study of Genesis. These are used to transfer the meanings of the Qabalah to linear language.

The meaning of each Aut on the following graph is determined by the number below it and depends first on whether it is a number from 1 to 9 or a multiple of 10 or 100; and second on the vertical and horizontal relationships of the number to the others on the graph. On pages 200 and 201, you will find a chart of the meanings of the Autiot from 1 to 9, which are known as the nine archetypes, and explanations of what these archetypes become when they are expressed as multiples of 10, 100, and 1,000. Key words in each meaning are in bold to help you recall them.

Example 1: The Aut Hay (5) signifies life (from the chart on page 200). The Aut Noun (50—a multiple of 10 and in relationship vertically to 5) signifies the existence of 5 (life). The Aut Khaf (500—a multiple of 100) signifies the cosmic state of 5 (life).

Example 2: Adam is Aleph (1), Dallet (4), Mem (40). If we substitute the meanings from the chart on page 200, Adam become the existence (40) of the spark of life (1) and resistance (4).

א	ב	ג	ד	ה	ו	ז	ח	ט
Aleph	Bayt Vayt	Ghimel	Dallet	Hay	Vav or Waw	Zayn	Hhayt	Tayt
1	2	3	4	5	6	7	8	9
י	כ	ל	מ	נ	ס	ע	פ	צ
Yod	Kaf Khaf	Lammed	Mem	Noun	Sammekh	Ayn	Pay Phay	Tsadde
10	20	30	40	50	60	70	80	90
ק	ר	ש	ת	ך	ם	ן	ף	ץ
Qof	Raysh	Seen Sheen	Tav	final Khaf	final Mem	final Noun	final Phay	final Tsadde
100	200	300	400	500	600	700	800	900

THE NINE ARCHETYPES

AUT	NUMBER	MEANING
Aleph	1	The unthinkable life-death pulsation of all that is and all that is not; the intermittant **spark of life** with no duration
Bayt (or Vayt)	2	The archetype of all **"dwellings,"** of all **containers,** the physical support without which nothing has form
Ghimel	3	The movement of every Bayt animated by Aleph; **tension**
Dallet	4	The existence, as response to life, of all that in nature is organically active with Ghimel. Where the structure is inorganic, Dallet is its own **resistance** to destruction.
Hay	5	The archetype of universal **life.** When it is conferred upon Dallet, it allows it to play the game of existence, in partnership with the intermittent life-death process.
Vav (or Waw)	6	Expresses the **fertilizing** agent, that which impregnates. It is the direct result of Hay upon Dallet.
Zayn	7	The achievement of every vital impregnation. This number opens the field of **every possible possibility; indetermination**
Hhayt	8	The sphere of storage of all undifferentiated energy or **unstructured substance or potential** It expresses the most unevolved state of energy, as opposed to its achieved freedom in Zayn.
Tayt	9	The archetype of the primeval **female building energy.** It draws its life from Hhayt and builds it gradually into structures.

THE ARCHETYPES AS MULTIPLES OF 10, 100, AND 1,000

- The nine Autiot from Yod (10) to Tsadde (90) describe the process of the nine archetypes in their factual, conditioned **existence.** Their projections in manifestation are always multiples of 10.

- The nine multiples of 100 express the exalted archetypes in their **cosmic states.**

- The number 1,000 is written with an enlarged Aleph. (In Hebrew, Aleph actually means one thousand, but is rarely used.) It expresses a **supreme power,** a tremendous cosmic energy, all pervading, timeless, unthinkable.

- The dotted lines from Khaf (20) to final Khaf (500), Mem (40) to final Mem (600), Noun (50) to final Noun (700), Phay (80) to final Phay (800), and Tsadde (90) to final Tsadde (900) signify expansion of human (the brain's) awareness—a movement from functioning at the existential level to functioning at the fully germinated, cosmic level.

Initially, these meanings will most likely confuse you because they have no references to cultural definitions. Remember, they are outside of time and space or cause and effect. They define patterns of energy very precisely. Studying the Qabalah is an exercise undertaken by the right hemisphere of the brain. Because we use the left hemisphere for processing literacy, the Qabalah represents a completely different way for us to process literate information. The symbols of the Qabalah, which are actually referred to as Aut (Autiot Yassod is the collective definition of all twenty-seven symbols), carry the patterns of how life's energy is manifested, both physically and potentially.

In order to begin your study, start with Genesis 1:1 and retranslate every word in the verse *at the letter level.* Begin with the first acronym, BRESYT (which has been translated as "In the beginning"). Write down each symbol and its corresponding number. Then study each separate symbol, using the definitions of the code in this appendix. Keep a notebook of your translations. Don't be discouraged if you seem to be getting nowhere. This is a very difficult system to master. As you concentrate on the first acronym, continue retranslating the rest of the text using the concordance. The trick is to keep on studying even when it seems as if nothing is happening. Simply by reading the text and retranslating each symbol your brain will begin to perceive patterns. But in order for the patterns to eventually be perceived, the brain must be subjected to repetition, just as Annie Sullivan kept at Helen despite Helen's resistance. Keep studying, regardless of seeming results. I studied intensively for nine months before my first breakthrough occurred. From then on it was much easier.

For further information on the Qabalah and the work of Carlos Suares, as well as that of other Qabalists, visit www.psyche.com.

Appendix 2

The Sacred Code
of the Alphabet

Note: All quoted material and graphics from Stan Tenen, the Meru Project (San Anselmo, Calif.: The Meru Foundation, 1994).

For all of science's achievements, the one thing it cannot do is create a living seed. It can manipulate seeds that already exist, as current genome projects demonstrate, but it cannot create a seed. Seed creation is the mystery of life.

Seeds and their properties—thus the pattern of life—were studied by the ancients, especially the Qabalists. The pattern of life is recognizable, but such knowledge, though it is the basis of everything living, is not even studied academically in modern times.

As I mention in the first chapter of this book, the functioning of the universal pattern of wholeness in the structure of the Hebrew letters of Genesis has been clarified by Stan Tenen, who has been working with the Hebrew alphabet for over twenty years. After first noticing a pattern in the letters, his studies led him to the discovery that this pattern reveals the significance of ancient geometries as representing successive steps in embryonic self-generation and self-organization, as that exemplified in seeds.

The work of his Meru Project is devoted to demonstrating that the letter text of Genesis is a model of evolution (which self-generated from seeds) and consciousness (which self-generated in the human brain). In this sense, the sacred code of the alphabet represents, as certain Jewish and Christian traditions claim, the pattern of creation, as well as being a technically meaningful archetype for the unfolding of conscious self-understanding in human awareness.

Tenen began his research by building models of the mathematical structure he discovered in the letters, which he now refers to as the Geometric Metaphor. This mathematical structure and metaphor accurately represents the self-organizing attributes of living, whole systems and is a perfect model of duality-in-unity, the pattern of integrated opposites so well demonstrated in seeds through the structure of germ and husk.

The Geometric Metaphor conveys the essence of the unfolding process of life—growth from seed to flower and the return to new seeds—which Tenen states is narrated so simply in Genesis 1:11: "And God said, Let the earth bring forth grass, the herb yielding seed, and the fruit tree yielding fruit after his kind, whose seed is in itself . . ." Such a model conveys the recursive, self-propagating, self-organizing property of living systems.

This process, presented geometrically, consists of an interdependent sequence of seven evolving geometric forms known as the Platonic and Archimedean solids—such as tetrahedra, cube, and octahedron—preceded by three preliminary dimensions of 0, 1, and 2—a point, line, and triangle. The whole of the Geometric Metaphor is revealed in the unfolding sequence of letters that make up the Hebrew text of Genesis.

By pairing off the letters in the first verse of Genesis and positioning them as beads on a simple bead string, then drawing it on paper, this is the diagram Tenen achieved:

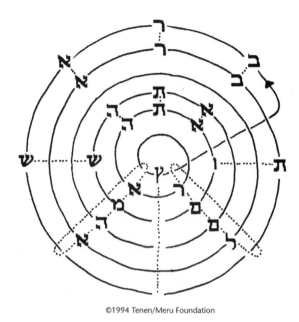

©1994 Tenen/Meru Foundation

Fig. 1. Genesis 1:1 on a bead string

When the defining element of this diagram is made into a three-dimensional model, it looks like this:

©1992 Tenen/Meru Foundation

Fig. 2. Flame structure

Its unique vortex shape is the most compact and most elegant representation of the sequence of letters of the first verse of Genesis in three-dimensional form, which cannot be fully appreciated until you see it like this:

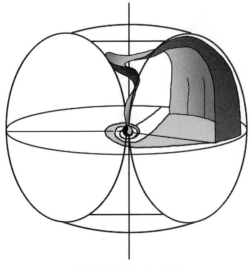

©1992 Tenen/Meru Foundation

Fig. 3. Axis Mundi

Other than being intrinsic to the structure of the Hebrew letters themselves, the flame structure generates and is at the foundation of a multitude of organic patterns, such as those shown in Figure 4, on the next page.

Tenen points out that each of the seven geometric models is composed of two opposing elements: one of symmetry, the other of no-symmetry. These two opposing elements are always complementary and mutually defining. There cannot be order (symmetry) without disorder (no-symmetry). Each endlessly begets the other as together they define the duality of nature: female and male, wave and particle, process and structure, cyclic and linear, continuous and discontinuous, germ and husk. This integration of opposites—symmetry and no-symmetry—is what creates the unity in the unified postulate revealed by Qabalah.

"The no-symmetry element," Tenen asserts, "is derived from the three-dimensional torus (a doughnut shape) that is topologically related to the vortex shape so prevalent in nature. The torus is the only form

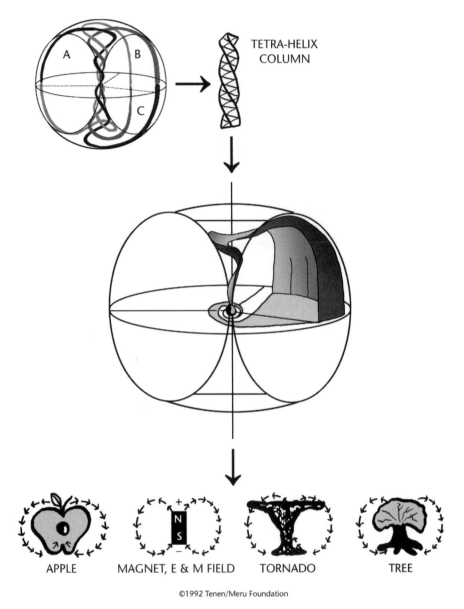

TETRA-HELIX
COLUMN

APPLE   MAGNET, E & M FIELD   TORNADO   TREE

©1992 Tenen/Meru Foundation

*Fig. 4. Generative pattern of flame structure. The tetra-helix column gives rise to
the structure of DNA, which is the foundation of all organic processes.*

that can maintain its integrity in a uniform medium and that can be
made of the 'material' of that medium" (which can be seen in the spi-
raling horns of animals such as antelope and bighorn sheep as well as

the shells of certain marine mollusks, such as the nautilus). The prevalence of the torus in nature was demonstrated by an article in the February 2002 issue of *Discover* magazine stating that sunspots are held together by potent magnetic fields that create a vortex, like a whirlpool, which is a portion of the torus.

Mathematicians have proved that a torus can be defined by a minimal seven-color map ribbon arranged as a spiral on its surface. The number 7 is, along with the number 9, a key element of Qabalic knowledge and intrinsic to the seven-day story of creation in the Genesis myth.

"This ribbon spiral," Tenen asserts, "can be considered the topological equivalent of the torus since it is the most economical, lowest-order definition of the torus." The ribbon-spiral form is a reciprocal (not a logarithmic) spiral. It matches the path of embryonic growth in nature. This image—of an organism that retains the successive phases of preceding growth—is that of our own body and brain. The body's structure, in the ontogeny-recapitulates-phylogeny pattern, reveals that a human fetus transits through all the stages of evolution during its nine months of gestation. The brain, with its four cortexes, also retains the successive phases of terrestrial evolution.

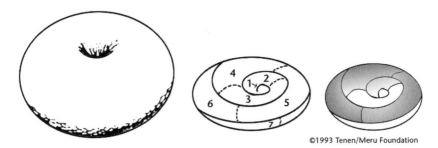

©1993 Tenen/Meru Foundation

Fig. 5. Ribbon spiral

In religious symbolism, Tenen suggests, the ribbon spiral serves as a model for the "idealized flame," and is also represented in the forms of the calla lily, menorah, dragon, and rainbow. It matches the spinal column in embryonic growth. You can see it under the Egyptian "Eye of

Horus," in Leonardo da Vinci's notebooks, and throughout The Book of Kells. The reciprocal spiral is the most asymmetrical spiral possible. This makes it a perfect complement to the completely symmetrical tetrahedron.

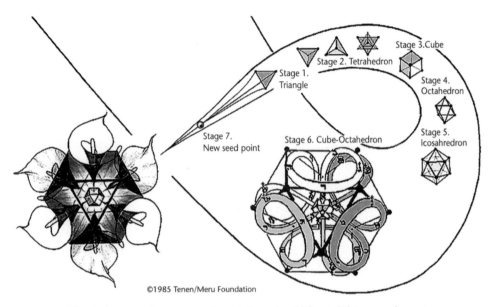

Fig. 6. A geometric representation of the cycle of life. At left is a configuration of seven lilies (including the one in the center). At right is the cube octohedron, the geometric representation of the seven lilies. Each lily produces a seed, which progresses through the seven stages of organic struture, represented by the seven Archimedean solids, as shown. Stage 1 is the triangle; stage 2 is the tetrahedron; stage 3 is the cube; stage 4 is the octahedron; stage 5 is the icosahedron; stage 6 is the cube octahedron; and stage 7 is the new seed point.

"The symmetry elements that model the stages of embryonic growth from seed to flower," states Tenen, "are the Platonic and Archimedean solids." They are used to illustrate the process of life evolving through the dimensions of form from the simplest organizational level to the most complex organizational level. Starting from the seed (point) and evolving to a triangular surface, the first solid—the tetrahedron—takes shape. The other solids then evolve from the tetrahedron, eventually unfolding into the cubic octahedron and finally the dodecahedron, the traditional Greek model for the universe.

"Each sequence," states Tenen, "of ten geometric forms (three preliminary and seven solids) constitutes one module in an infinite, recursive hierarchy. This infinite, recursive hierarchy is the geometric metaphor for life and represents a universal language based upon the topology of self-reference."

The first thing Tenen noticed about the vortex shape generated by the first verse of Genesis is that it looks like a flame. Fire and flame are often associated with consciousness, especially in ancient texts. But more important for our investigation, they are manifestations of light. "When the elements for symmetry and no-symmetry are brought together, as they always are in nature, they form the geometric model of, among other things, the flame in the vessel, which is one essential symbol of Islam, or the Genie in the lamp in the myth of Aladdin."

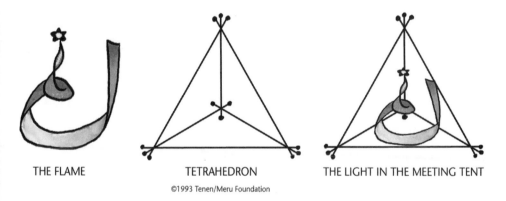

THE FLAME TETRAHEDRON THE LIGHT IN THE MEETING TENT

©1993 Tenen/Meru Foundation

Fig. 7. At left is the flame structure, which, on the right, is shown contained within the tetrahedron. The metaphor of the flame in the tent refers to spirit in body, germ within the structure of the husk—our dual nature.

A flame is asymmetrical, as is the vine, tree, or plant that emerges from a germ. A tetrahedron is the model of symmetry because it represents the most compact form of structural symmetry in three dimensions. The flame and its vessel, or germ and its husk, are complementary and mutually defining. There cannot be tetrahedral symmetry/order without the disorder of asymmetrical flames as defining contrasts. The letters of the ancient sacred alphabets are produced when the asymmetric "flame" is viewed through the symmetries of the tetrahedron-shaped "vessel."

A flame represents spirit, or the generative juice of growth, a hyper-dimensional aspect of life. The tetrahedron represents form, the three-dimensional aspect of organic structure. A "flame within a tent" is the same image as "spirit within form." We experience this "miraculous" occurrence every day as the "fire" of perception (or awareness) within the vessel of the body. This is the mystery and fact of process wedded to form: wave to particle, consciousness to physical being, germ to husk.

When we have a transcendental experience, it is nonsensory (hyperdimensional). Because it is nonsensory, we say that it is mystical, for we usually process information through our senses. Yet we are all capable of this nonsensory, transcendental way of processing. If we want to share such experiences with others, we must give people the means to re-create these experiences, such as yoga, chant, meditation, or a book of scriptures.

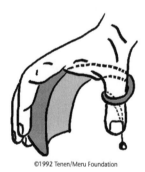

©1992 Tenen/Meru Foundation

Fig. 8. Flame in hand

Tenen knew that turning over a three-dimensional shape in the mind (hyperspace) constitutes a kind of "yoga" and can create a transcendental experience. But it is very difficult to do. Yet these Hebrew letters in Genesis have another astonishing aspect that allows them to be "turned over" in any direction so as to be visualized by the mind in any position: The original vortex shape fits perfectly to the human hand.

Hold the hand in several meditative positions, and you re-create the sacred alphabet.

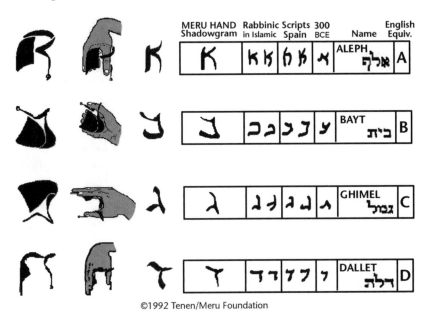

©1992 Tenen/Meru Foundation

Fig. 9. These hand positions represent a possible way that the continuity of the Qabalic language was maintained before written language emerged.

Tenen states, "The human hand is very special. It is possible we are named 'human' from the Latin word for hand, *manus*. The part of the brain that controls hand movements also contains Broca's and Wernicke's regions, which control speech. Studies have shown that nonhearing children make use of the same neural maps, and learn sign language in almost the same fashion as hearing children learn spoken language. Articulations and gestures of our hands correspond to the essential elements of our speech as we produce and process them in our minds. Indeed, most of us cannot talk without using our hands."

But more important, our hands and our speech—when combined in the written word—are the means by which we express our purely personal internal thoughts to the external physical world. Our hands—when used to express the contents of the mind through written symbols—are the embodiment of the generative impulse that is at the heart of all creation. Through writing, our hands are the medium by which we project the unseen, nonmaterial contents of our consciousness—the flame—into physicality—the vessel. They are also the means by which we project the dimensions of physicality into our consciousness through the written symbols representing it, which the mind processes as information.

The geometric metaphor in the Hebrew letters represents the same model of unity as the Qabalic code in Genesis. Thus, Tenen affirms, the text of Genesis is coded at the letter level with the pattern of whole-systems creation, just as ancient sources claim. Qabalah is merely another name for this pattern, which is *the* pattern of life.

Tenen made a model of the original vortex shape inside its "tent/vessel" and projected its shadow onto a wall. By changing the angle of the model, different letters of the Hebrew alphabet were projected as shadows on the wall until all twenty-seven appeared.

This led Tenen to ask rhetorically, "If there are coded patterns embedded in the Biblical text, how could they have survived over thousands of years?"

His geometric models show the presence of an error-correcting pattern in the sequence of Hebrew letters/symbols that is independent of the linguistic translation. He asserts that every letter in the Hebrew Bible sequence is determined by the geometric model. Tenen researched canonized and non-canonized versions of the Bible and discovered that canonized versions always contain the letter sequence that produces the Geometric Metaphor whereas non-canonized versions (such as that of the Samaritans) don't, even if they contain the same words, because those words are spelled differently from those in the canonized versions.

He further asks, "How is it possible to write the Bible story when under the constraints imposed by an underlying pattern of letters produced from a geometrical model?"

To comprehend how this can be, we must realize that unlike modern English, early Hebrew writing had few limitations or grammatical rules. One fact that supports this idea is that there were no written vowel sounds in the early texts. Vowel sounds were created later by adding vocalization symbols—little curlicues and accents (diacritical marks) placed underneath, above, or beside the original symbols. In other words, the original written document was much more than a simple linguistic text. Supporting such a thesis, anthropologists have found that the runic characters of the Norse language, as well as Celtic symbols, appear to have served sacred and spiritual purposes for hundreds of years prior to their application as written and/or linguistic symbols.

There are many clues sprinkled throughout the text of Genesis that characterize the true nature of the sacred coded alphabet. For instance, the first verse of Genesis uses twenty-eight letters—that is, twenty-seven letters plus the twenty-seventh letter of this twenty-seven–symbol system. This led Tenen to count the Hebrew symbols, not by tens, as we commonly do today, and not by twos, as do digital computers, but by threes, or base 3: 3 x 3 x 3 = 27. There are nine stations on the graph of Qabalah. The basis of Christianity is a trinity.

Tenen's work demonstrates previously hidden knowledge pertaining to Genesis, and perhaps to all of our sacred scriptures. Neither theologians nor biblical scholars are aware of this knowledge. Because it is outside the domain of language, it is outside the domain of theology or biblical scholarship. If we wish to comprehend this knowledge, we must go beyond language to discover it. Moving beyond language forces the brain into areas it is neither aware of nor comfortable with. Yet this knowledge is vital to our continued evolution as a species, and to the brain's self-organization of information.

Bibliography

The Bible, King James Version.

Campbell, Joseph. *Transformations of Myth Through Time.* New York: Harper & Row, 1990.

———. *Historical Atlas of World Mythology.* Vol. 2, *The Way of the Seeded Earth.* Part II, *Mythologies of the Primitive Planters, The Northern Americas.* New York: Harper & Row, 1989.

Damasio, Antonio. *Descartes' Error: Emotion, Reason and the Human Brain.* New York: Avon Books, 1995.

Eisler, Riane. *Sacred Pleasure: Sex, Myth and the Politics of the Body—New Paths to Power and Love.* San Francisco: HarperSanFrancisco, 1996.

Estes, Clarissa Pinkola. *Women Who Run With the Wolves: Myths and Stories of the Wild Woman Archetype.* New York: Ballantine Books, 1992.

Fox, Matthew. *Original Blessing.* San Francisco: Bear & Company Publishing, 1983.

Goldberg, Elkhonon. *The Executive Brain: Frontal Lobes and the Civilized Mind.* Oxford University Press, 2001.

Goleman, Daniel. *Emotional Intelligence: Why It Can Matter More Than IQ.* New York: Bantam Books, 1995.

Greenspan, Stanley. *The Growth of the Mind and the Endangered Origins of Intelligence.* Reading, Mass.: Perseus Books, 1998.

Hanford, Rob. "Plane Sense, Baseball, and the Pythagorean Theorem: An In-Depth Study of Indo-European Worldview." Master's thesis, University of California, Berkeley, 1979.

Heinlein, Robert. *Stranger in a Strange Land*. New York: Putnam, 1961.

MacLean, Paul D. *The Triune Brain in Evolution: Role in Paleocerebral Functions*. New York: Plenum Press, 1990.

———. "A Triune Concept of the Brain and Behavior." In the *Hincks Memorial Lectures*. Edited by Thomas J. Boag and Dougal Campbell. Toronto: University of Toronto Press, 1973.

Pearce, Joseph Chilton. *Evolution's End: Claiming the Potential of Our Intelligence*. San Francisco: HarperSanFrancisco, 1992.

Scott, Mary Hugh. *The Passion of Being Woman: A Love Story from the Past for the Twenty-First Century*. Aspen, Colo.: MacMurray and Beck Communications, 1991.

Shlain, Leonard. *The Alphabet Versus the Goddess: The Conflict Between Word and Image*. New York, Viking, 1998

———. *Art and Physics: Parallel Visions in Space, Time and Light*. New York: William Morrow & Co., 1991.

Strong, James. *The Exhaustive Concordance of the Bible*. Madison, N.J., 1894.

Suares, Carlo. *The Cipher of Genesis: The Original Code of Qabala as Applied to the Scriptures*. York Beach, Maine: Samuel Weiser, 1994.

———. *The Qabala Trilogy*. Boston: Shambhala Publications, 1985.

Toynbee, Arnold. *A Study of History*. New York: Weathervane Books, 1972.

Vogler, Christopher. *The Writer's Journey: Mythic Structure for Storytellers and Screenwriters*. Studio City, Calif.: Michael Wiese Productions Book, 1992.

Weisman, Alan. *Gaviotas: A Village to Reinvent the World*. White River Junction, Vt.: Chelsea Green, 1998.

Young, Arthur. *The Geometry of Meaning*. New York: Delacorte Press, 1979.

———. *The Reflexive Universe: Evolution of Consciousness*. New York: Delacorte Press, 1979.

Zajonc, Arthur. *Catching the Light: The Intertwining of Light and Mind*. Oxford University Press, 1995.

BOOKS OF RELATED INTEREST

THE BIOLOGY OF TRANSCENDENCE
A Blueprint of the Human Spirit
by Joseph Chilton Pearce

THE CRACK IN THE COSMIC EGG
New Constructs of Mind and Reality
by Joseph Chilton Pearce

A NEW SCIENCE OF LIFE
The Hypothesis of Morphic Resonance
by Rupert Sheldrake

CHAOS, CREATIVITY, AND COSMIC CONSCIOUSNESS
by Rupert Sheldrake, Terence McKenna, and Ralph Abraham

THE DOUBLE GODDESS
Women Sharing Power
by Vicki Noble

THE GREAT GODDESS
Reverence of the Divine Feminine from the Paleolithic to the Present
by Jean Markale

THE KABBALAH OF THE SOUL
The Transformative Psychology and Practices of Jewish Mysticism
by Leonora Leet, Ph.D.

THE SECRET DOCTRINE OF THE KABBALAH
Recovering the Key to Hebraic Sacred Science
by Leonora Leet, Ph.D.

Inner Traditions • Bear & Company
P.O. Box 388
Rochester, VT 05767
1-800-246-8648
www.InnerTraditions.com

Or contact your local bookseller